the miniaturists

Minia

BARBARA

the miniaturists

....

Barbara Browning

DUKE UNIVERSITY PRESS · DURHAM AND LONDON · 2022

Designed by Matthew Tauch
Typeset in Garamond Premier Pro by Copperline Book Services

Library of Congress Cataloging-in-Publication Data
Names: Browning, Barbara, [date] author.
Title: The miniaturists / Barbara Browning.
Description: Durham : Duke University Press, 2022. |
Includes bibliographical references.
Identifiers: LCCN 2022005852 (print)
LCCN 2022005853 (ebook)
ISBN 9781478016274 (hardcover)
ISBN 9781478018919 (paperback)
ISBN 9781478023548 (ebook)
Subjects: LCSH: Miniature objects in literature. | Literature—
History and criticism. | BISAC: BIOGRAPHY & AUTOBIOGRAPHY /
Historical | SOCIAL SCIENCE / Gender Studies
Classification: LCC PN56.M5368 B769 2022 (print) |
LCC PN56.M5368 (ebook) | DDC 814/.54—dc23/eng/20220611
LC record available at https://lccn.loc.gov/2022005852
LC ebook record available at https://lccn.loc.gov/2022005853

Cover art: Frances Glessner Lee, Nutshell Studies of
Unexplained Death, *Kitchen* (detail), c. 1944–46. Collection
of the Harvard Medical School, Harvard University, Cambridge, MA.
Photo by Lorie Shaull.

for Leo

contents

....

foibles of insects and men

....

I t all began as a question of feminist methodology.

A friend of mine had written a book about archiving. In it, she mentioned a fellow student in graduate school who had told her about "vaginal libraries"—this, in reference to Argentine women imprisoned during the dictatorship, who hid dissident texts in their private parts. My friend had extended this figure to consider various ways in which women store certain information in their bodies. I was trying to come up with a word for this messy, interesting process, which I wanted to term *gynarchivism*. So first I Googled *gynarchy*, which literally means government by women but is most frequently used to refer to insect societies dominated by females.

I was quickly directed to a seemingly obscure text by William Morton Wheeler titled *Social Life among the Insects* (1923). The brief passage that popped up was weirdly captivating. In it, Wheeler notes that certain species have succeeded in "reducing the male to a mere episode in the life of the female."

During the singular act of mating in these insects—a prodigious one-night stand—sperm is deposited in the female's spermatheca, "a small muscular sac" that supplies glandular secretions that can preserve the sperm, alive, indefinitely. "According to a generally accepted theory," Wheeler writes, "the female can voluntarily contract the wall of her spermatheca and thus permit sperm to leave it and fertilize the eggs as they are passing its orifice on their way to being laid, or she can keep the orifice closed and thus lay unfertilized eggs." That is, she can perform birth control just by clenching her spermatheca when she's ovulating. In fact, she can even determine the sex of her offspring, as her unfertilized eggs can still produce males if she wants them. "We are justified," Wheeler continues, "in regarding the female parasitoid, wasp, bee or ant, after she has appropriated and stored in her spermatheca all the essential elements of the male [!!!], as a potential hermaphrodite" (47–48).

At this point, Wheeler waxes poetic—or, to be more accurate, his account begins to sound something like a Hitchcock film: "In the solitary wasps the male is a nonentity, although in a few species he may hang around and try to guard the nest. But in the bees, ants and social wasps he has not even the status of a loafing policeman, and all the activities of the community are carried on by the females, and mostly by widows, debutantes and spinsters." He concludes the passage: "The facts certainly compel even those who, like myself, are neither feminists nor vegetarians, to confess that the whole trend of evolution in the most interesting of social insects is towards an ever increasing matriarchy, or gynarchy and vegetarianism" (48).

Needless to say, I immediately ordered the book on interlibrary loan.

* * *

I should pause here to tell you that I live with an amateur naturalist. This was not an obvious turn of events in my life. We met when I was in my fifties, he in his sixties, and when he first invited me to visit his little cottage in the countryside of Normandy, I warned him that I was something like the Eva Gabor character in the old sitcom *Green Acres*. Being French, he had no idea what I was talking about. Actually, if you're not of my vintage, perhaps that will also go over your head. *Green Acres* was the zany tale of a Manhattan lawyer who decided to give up the rat race of city life and live in the country. His glamorous Eastern European wife was trying to give it a go, but under protest. In the opening credits, she'd habitually remind her hubby:

New York is where I'd rather stay
I get allergic smelling hay
I just adore a penthouse view
Dah-ling, I love you, but give me Park Avenue

Well, I'm neither Eastern European nor particularly glamorous, and expensive apartments on Park Avenue tend to make me very uncomfortable, but it was true that I'd been residing happily in New York for over a quarter of a century and didn't have much experience with—or appetite for—country living.

S, on the other hand, was born in Paris and lived there for most of his life, with occasional sojourns in other parts of the world. He wasn't a lawyer—far from it. He was a hand-to-mouth singer/songwriter and freelance screenwriter. But like Eva Gabor's TV husband, he abandoned urbanity in his forties and decamped to what I sometimes call his Hobbit House in a little hamlet called Pourry. When I went there, I was charmed. In the daylight hours, the birds sang and the breeze whistled through the trees, but at night it was utterly silent. I found myself sleeping eleven hours at a stretch. There was a forest nearby, where S would forage for baby toads and salamander larvae, which he tended to in a couple of large glass boxes in the house, furnishing them with moss, muck, beetles, and slugs.

Once we decided to cohabitate, our time was mostly spent at the New York apartment, where each of us had a workspace for writing. But whenever my teaching schedule allowed it, we'd hightail it to the house in Normandy. In the country, we maintained a similar schedule of solitary writing days, punctuated by meals and occasional walks together. But we slept more. I should say, we sleep more. I'm writing this from the garden in Pourry.

* * *

When I received my copy of *Social Life among the Insects*, there were more surprises. On the very first page, Wheeler salutes "Prince Kropotkin"! That won't come as such a surprise to you if you know that Kropotkin was also a naturalist, but in citing his observations regarding "mutual aid" in nature, as a necessary corrective or at least complement to Darwinian theory, Wheeler goes on to argue for the postwar impulse "towards ever greater solidarity, of general disarmament, of a drawing together not only of men to men, but of nations to nations throughout the world, of a recasting and refinement of all our economic, political, social, educational and religious activities for the purposes of greater mutual helpfulness" (5).

As for that disavowal of his own feminism, I wondered about his sincerity. In snooping around some more on the internet, I discovered that he appeared to return habitually in his writings (which were copious) to what he called "the problem of the male." In a 1933 address to the American Society of Naturalists (published in the *Scientific Monthly* in 1934), he noted "the high degree of integration and stability of the insect society and the extraordinarily harmonious and self-sacrificing cooperation of its individual members, as contrasted with the mobility, instability, and mutual aggressiveness so conspicuous among the members of our own society." Among many species, including our own, Wheeler claimed that his own sex might be "properly called the antisocial sex" (292–93).

The disavowal of vegetarianism, however, appeared to be true—and yet, again, it followed the logic of many insects.

Regarding the life of the female, things really came to a head in a passage of *Social Life* in which Wheeler presented the parable of the *Sphex* wasps, as he put it,

in the form of a tragic drama in three acts, with the following brief synopsis:

Act I. A sandy country with sparse vegetation inhabited by caterpillars and other insects. Time, a hot, sunny day in early August. Scene 1. Miss Sphex arrayed in all the charm of maidenhood being courted by Mr. Sphex. Wedding among the flowers. Scene 2. Mrs. Sphex, deserted by her scatter-brained spouse, settles down and excavates a kind of cyclone-cellar. She closes its door and leaves the stage.

Act II. Scene 1. Same as in Act I. Mrs. Sphex, hunting in the vegetation, finds a caterpillar, struggles with it, stings it and gnaws its neck till it lies motionless. Scene 2. She drags it into the cellar and placing her offspring on it behind the scenes, returns and at once leaves the stage after locking the door, amid a storm of applause.

Act III. Scene 1. Interior of Mrs. Sphex's cellar. Baby Sphex slowly devouring caterpillar till only its skin remains. Scene 2. Baby Sphex, now a large, buxom lass, weaves an elaborate nightgown for herself and goes to bed as the curtain falls. (56)

Despite its electrifying plot and *mise-en-scène,* Wheeler himself declares this drama "defective" in Aristotelian terms because the climax comes too soon, with the heroine abandoning the stage to her "drowsy offspring" in the third act. So he proposes a revision, in which the third act replaces the first, with the first and second acts becoming the second and third. Thus, the daughter becomes the central figure, and we follow her gradual transformation from infancy, through a troubled marriage and desertion, to her heroic excavation of the cellar, and concluding with "the thrilling chase, stinging and entombment of the hereditary victim in the third act" (57).

Medea, anyone?

Wheeler admits to having committed the "unpardonable sin" of anthropomorphizing the wasp but asks for a little more patience from his reader as he proceeds to "vespize" the human being: "Suppose that the human mother were in the habit of carefully tying her new-born baby to the arm-pit of a paralyzed elephant which she had locked in a huge cellar." Um, okay.

> The baby—we must, of course, suppose that it is a girl baby—is armless, legless and blind but has been born with powerful jaws and teeth and an insatiable appetite. Under the circumstances she would have to eat the elephant or die. Supposing now that she fed on the elephant day after day between naps till only its tough hide and hard skeleton were left, and that she then took an unusually long nap and awoke as a magnificent, winged, strong-limbed amazon, with a marvelously keen sense of smell and superb eyes, clad in burnished armor and with a poisoned lance in her hand. With such attractions and equipment we could hardly expect her to stay long in a cellar. She would at once break through the soil into the daylight. Now suppose she happened to emerge, with a great and natural appetite, in a zoological garden, should we be astonished to see her make straight for the elephant house? Why, she would recognize the faintest odor of elephant borne to her on the breeze. She would herself be, in a sense, merely a metabolized elephant. Of course, we should be startled to see her leap on the elephant's back, plunge her lance into its armpit, drag it several miles over the ground, hide it in a cellar, and tie her offspring to its hide. (57–58)

All of this is ostensibly laid out in order to illustrate an argument regarding larval "memory," though it seems to me entirely suited for the making of an action film or a Marvel comic.

* * *

I should mention yet another reason I was drawn to William Morton Wheeler—although at this point you may be wondering who wouldn't be. I was at the time (and in fact still am) directing the dissertation of a young woman who was writing on anarcha-feminism, and she had proposed a chapter on "anarchist beekeeping" as a case study. Actually, the beekeeper in question would refute that term, since he didn't "keep" bees but cohabitated with them, never seeking to organize their behavior, since they seemed to have their own perfectly functional way of doing things. In fact, he didn't even call them "bees" but rather "apian beings." It perhaps goes without saying that this nomenclature was an effort to not privilege human ontology over that of the insects. It perhaps also goes without saying that he was something of an outlier in the world of bee enthusiasts. I'm not sure if he considered himself an anarcha-feminist, though my student did. Actually, I have a feeling that he was the kind of person who avoided all manners of isms, which is also true of S. Somewhat like my student, I have the perhaps irritating habit of ignoring his disavowals, just as I was ignoring those of William Morton Wheeler.

You may also be wondering about the political efficacy or wisdom of doing this. I assure you that the question has crossed my mind as well.

* * *

After devouring *Social Life among the Insects*, I ordered a few more books. My appetite was something like that of a strong-limbed amazon catching a whiff of succulent elephant. Still, there was no question of consuming Wheeler's entire oeuvre, colossal as it was, and most of it out of print. The first vintage volume to arrive was actually not a book by him but a biography of Wheeler published by Harvard University Press in 1970. It was authored by Mary Alice Evans and Howard Ensign Evans, the latter being an esteemed entomologist himself. Apparently, Howard was the scientific fact-checker, and his wife, Mary Alice, was responsible for much of the personal narrative in the book. The picture that began to emerge in this account of Wheeler's life was a little confusing.

His early life was simultaneously predictable and exceptional: he was born in Milwaukee (I was also born in Wisconsin!) in 1865, and he displayed an early fascination with bugs. His parents sent him to a German academy (according to him, on account of his "bad behavior"), where he learned to read not only German, but also French, Spanish, Italian, Greek, and Latin (his writings are jam-packed with epigraphs and citations from classical literature, all in the original languages). He worked as a specimen handler in a natural science museum in upstate New York, returned briefly to Milwaukee, and then went to Clark University, where he wrote a doctoral dissertation on insect embryology. He held a number of positions at different academic institutions and major museums, finally settling at Harvard, and several of his students would go on to achieve renown—among them, interestingly, Alfred Kinsey.

There were some discreet references in this biography to Wheeler's intimate life. He was betrothed to a childhood sweetheart who apparently dumped him. Then he got engaged to her sister. That also didn't work out (no clue as to why), but Wheeler maintained good relations with both the sisters, and years later he visited them with his wife, Dora.

In the passages regarding his relations with his colleagues and students, Wheeler sometimes appeared affable and fatherly, sometimes shy. But occasionally he sounded like a pedantic bully. I was intrigued by the number of female, African American, and Asian scholars whom he both trained and worked with, but when I followed the leads on some of these connections, they were disconcerting. One of his female students went on to work for a eugenicist organization. Of course, one can't always hold the teacher responsible for the student's proclivities.

Wheeler's wife, Dora Wheeler, née Emerson, was politically active in food distribution, and she campaigned for Herbert Hoover. I also found this a little disconcerting, though it seems her enthusiasm was based on Hoover's own activities in international food aid during the war, when he was considered a progressive. Dora's interest in food distribution appears to have been linked to Wheeler's study of the phenomenon among ants.

I was curious about the relationship between Mary Alice and Howard Evans. I paused in my reading of their book and found this in a memorial penned by a student of Howard's, Mary Jane West-Eberhard, after his death:

> Howard Evans and Mary Alice Dietrich were married in 1954, soon after Mary Alice had finished her Ph.D. in science education at Cornell and not long after Howard had returned to work there as assistant professor of entomology in 1952.... Mary Alice was the daughter of the Cornell entomologist Henry Dietrich, who had "warned his daughters to stay away from entomologists, who were likely to be impecunious and

little appreciated by society." "Fortunately," Howard wrote, "Mary Alice failed to take his advice." (123)

When I mentioned this to S, he asked me if I knew Donovan's "Song of the Naturalist's Wife." He played it for me. It's a gentle song, in which a wife wonders if it's her husband she sees toddling toward her from his day by the sea. "Do I see your buckets full / Buckets full of shells?" She thinks she recognizes him from afar, with his "weary weave," his slow, distracted way of meandering home.

S doesn't go to the seaside for his collecting. He has a mucky pond in the forest that he likes to visit with a bucket and a net. But, indeed, when he's coming back from his excursions, slightly bent under his straw hat, you might describe his gait as a weary weave.

* * *

Although it was the story of Ms. Sphex that really hooked me, most of Wheeler's monographs are in the subfield of myrmecology—the study of ants. Ants are the focus of the second half of *Social Life among the Insects,* and again, Wheeler doesn't hesitate to compare their social behavior to our own. In a chapter on parasitism, he comes up with a colorful list of terms to describe the different ways in which ants act as both parasites and hosts. In the former category, he offers alternative names for the Latinate ones employed by most myrmecologists (cleptobiosis, lestobiosis, plesiobiosis, parabiosis, xenobiosis, and dulosis): brigandage, thievery, neighborliness, tutelage, hospitality, and "slavery" (there is no indication of why this last term is put in scare quotes). In the latter category, the scientific designations (synechthrans, synoeketes, commensals, and symphiles) are rendered: persecuted intruders, indifferently tolerated guests, messmates, and true guests.

It's another classic case of anthropomorphizing, of course, but predictably, Wheeler flips things around to consider the human species, which "furnishes the most striking illustrations of the case with which both the parasitic and host rôles may be assumed by a social animal":

> Our bodies, our domestic animals and food plants, dwellings, stored foods, clothing and refuse support such numbers of greedy organisms, and we parasitize on one another to such an extent that the biologist marvels how the race can survive. We not only tolerate but even foster in our midst whole parasitic trades, institutions, castes and nations, hordes of bureaucrats, grafting politicians, middlemen, profiteers and usurers, a vast and varied assortment of criminals, hoboes, defectives, prostitutes, white-slavers and other purveyors to antisocial proclivities, in a word so many non-productive, food-consuming and space-occupying parasites that their support absorbs nearly all the energy of the independent members of society. This condition is, of course, responsible for the small amount of free creative activity in many nations. (197–98)

While you might find the general thrust of the passage to have some validity, perhaps you, like me, will balk at some of the names on Wheeler's list. I don't think I need to say which ones or why. Indeed, at the end of the passage, Wheeler himself says (this chapter was originally delivered as a public lecture): "I have expressed myself somewhat drastically on human parasitism. If I attempted to utter all my opinions on the subject I should probably not be permitted to survive till the next lecture, even in so tolerant a community as Boston" (198).

He does go on to tell a story about the relations between ants and the minuscule mites they sometimes host in their colonies. It seems the tiny mite might have certain "glandular attractions" that can "induce the ants to adopt, feed and care for it and thus become a member of the colony, just as an attractive and apparently well-behaved foreigner can secure naturalization and nourishment in any human community" (221). Well, would that that were so, but I continue:

> Perhaps we can best appreciate the relations of the ants to the mites if we fancy ourselves blind, condemned to live in dark cellars, and continually occupied with pasturing and milking fat, sluggish cows, yielding quantities of strained honey instead of milk. Then let us suppose that, occasionally, there alighted on our cheeks or backs small creatures which, by placing themselves in positions symmetrical to the median longitudinal axis of our bodies, took great care not to annoy us and stretched forth to us from time to time small, soft hands, like those of our friends, begging for a little honey, should we not, under the circumstances, treat these little Old Men of the Sea with much lenity and even with something akin to affection? (227)

The scenario was touching. Still, I must say that there were several moments in my reading of *Social Life among the Insects* that left me ill at ease.

* * *

Perhaps you're wondering about that anarcha-feminist student of mine. Her name is Sarah. She took a little time off from writing about the bee enthusiast to do some organizing work in Greece. She's currently living in a semipublic artists' space, helping to set up a free-form feminist library for other anarchists and migrants. Well, if I said that one can't always hold the teacher responsible for a student's unsavory proclivities, I should also note that a teacher really can't take credit for the savory ones. Still, I can't help feeling a little proud.

* * *

S has been pleased to see me sitting in the garden these past few days working on this story about an entomologist. Yesterday, he came outside with two of his favorite childhood books to show me. Odette Vincent-Fumet wrote and illustrated them, and they were published in Montreal in 1942. They were part of a series of three volumes: *Pluck—ses aventures, Pluck—chez les fourmis,* and *Pluck—chez les abeilles.* S had only the second and third volumes. These books are fairly obscure, and he's not sure where his parents found them. Even my vigorous internet research yielded little information on the series and their author. They were printed on a letterpress, with the words in blue ink and the illustrations in red. Since we're missing the first volume, I'm not sure exactly how Pluck, a miniature boy in striped leggings and a matching stocking cap, ended up having all these adventures with the ants and bees. There's a didactic premise to the series, as the insects instruct Pluck in their ways of doing things. But there's also a love story woven throughout: Pluck encounters a miniature girl named Fleurette who was kidnapped by the ants in her infancy, and he aims to get her back home. They lose each other at various points as Pluck does battle with spiders and various other predators, but at the end of *Pluck—chez les abeilles* he finds her again, back home with her family, *"bien grandie et embellie,"* "all grown up and beautified." She says she's missed him while he was gone, and she asks him not to go on any more adventures with the insects. He doesn't want to make any promises but tells her that if he does go, she should wait for him. Then he says, *"Alors, si vous vouliez, quand je serai fixé ici définitivement, nous nous marierons?"* "So, if you want, when I'm permanently installed here, we'll get married?" (45). Fleurette answers by throwing herself into his arms.

* * *

Apparently, William Morton Wheeler also believed in romantic love. In that chapter on ant parasitism, he quotes L. T. Hobhouse, an early proponent of social liberalism, on the topic: "After all, is an ant-nourishing parasite that destroys its young guilty of a greater absurdity than, say a mother promoting her daughter's happiness by selling her to a rich husband . . . ? The mother really desires her daughter's happiness, but her conception of the means thereto is confused, and rendered self-contradictory by worldly ambitions" (23).

Hobhouse was basing his argument on the research of Erich Wasmann, an entomologist and Jesuit priest. In a lengthy endnote on this citation, Wheeler says that Wasmann

has recently published an elaborate résumé of his 35 years of investigation of Lomechusini and other myrmecophiles, largely as a criticism of and counterblast to my paper on the study of ant larvae (1918). As a study in Jesuit psychology the work may be recommended to biologists who can spare the time for its perusal from more important occupations. He has to admit the facts cited in my paper and much of my interpretation of them, but by adroit perversion of my statements, hairsplitting definitions and subtleties and by the production of voluminous smoke-screens of Thomistic argumentation he seeks to conceal the real scientific weakness of his contentions. (344n10)

The note goes on with a few more zingers about Wasmann's shortcomings, largely attributed to his religious inclinations, but also to his commitment to genetics.

Erich Wasmann once wrote a book celebrating the contributions of Hildegard von Bingen to the natural sciences.

The indexer of *Social Life among the Insects* confused Erich Wasmann with August Weismann, also cited extensively by Wheeler. August Weismann was the Jewish evolutionary biologist who developed germ plasm theory. Germ plasm theory counters the Lamarckian thesis that an organism can pass on characteristics that it has acquired through use or disuse during its lifetime to its offspring. Weismann disproved this theory by cutting off the tails of mice for twenty-two successive generations, with no change in inheritance. Isaac Asimov later pointed out that the circumcision of Jewish boys over many more generations than that should have made the experiment moot.

But I was talking about romantic love. Wheeler didn't mind citing Hobhouse citing Wasmann in that little passage about why mothers shouldn't marry off their beloved daughters to rich men in hopes of making them happy.

I don't think Mary Alice Evans's father was serious when he tried to warn her and her sister off marrying an impecunious entomologist.

* * *

For the last two nights, S and I have tiptoed out of the house to watch a hedgehog nibbling at the dinner scraps we left by the front door. I'd never seen a hedgehog up close. It was adorable. S gently poured some milk into a saucer and placed it nearby. In the morning, the milk was gone. Same thing the second night. S is happy like a ten-year-old kid.

* * *

William Morton Wheeler had little patience for the "rose-colored psychologies of the academic type," which he felt "confine[d their] attention to the head and upper extremities and drape[d] or ignore[d] the other parts" (cited in Evans and Evans, 226). Real psychoanalysts, however, were, to his mind, "getting down to brass tacks." Sigmund Freud and his more committed followers, he said,

> have had the courage to dig up the subconscious, that hotbed of all the egotism, greed, lust, pugnacity, cowardice, sloth, hate, and envy which every single one of us carries about as his inheritance from the animal world. These are all ethically and aesthetically very unpleasant phenomena but they are just as real and fundamental as our entrails, blood, and reproductive organs. In this matter, I am glad to admit, the theologians, with their doctrine of total depravity, seem to me to be nearer

the truth than the psychologists. I should say, however, that our depravity is only about 85 to 90%.

Wheeler said this in an address to the Royce Club in May 1917. He went on:

> If Freud told us, as he probably would if he were here, that all of us who have been smoking this evening have merely been exhibiting a surviving nutritional infantilism with the substitution of cigars for our mothers' breasts, we should, of course, exclaim, like some New England farmer confronted with a wildly improbable statement, *Gosh!* But after all, is the substitution by a man of a roll of dried *Nicotiana* leaves for a woman's breast any more preposterous than the Empidid's substitution of a balloon of salivary bubbles for a juicy fly ... ? (227–28)

In preparation for this talk, or at least in thinking through the question of "instincts," Wheeler claims to have "read some twenty volumes of psychoanalytic literature comprising the works of [Sigmund] Freud, [Carl] Jung, [Abraham] Brill, [Alfred] Adler, Ernest Jones, [Sándor] Ferenczi, [Poul] Bjerre, and W. A. White, with the result that I feel as if I had been taking a course of swimming lessons in a veritable cesspool of learning" (226).

S also loves Ferenczi, particularly *Thalassa: A Theory of Genitality* (1924), which argues that coitus represents a kind of phylogenetic nostalgia for the sea life from which man emerged. He (S, that is) was in psychoanalysis for years, and I don't think he regrets it, though it didn't prevent a later episode of depression. But of course that's not really what psychoanalysis is for.

In 1925, Wheeler wrote another scathing appraisal of what he considered the lightweight, "rose-colored" behaviorist psychology of John B. Watson, an "obstreperous youngster" who "has been so frequently spanked that he has by this time undoubtedly developed ischial callosities of some thickness" (cited in Evans and Evans, 229). This review was published in Raymond Pearl's *Quarterly Review of Biology.* Pearl, a friend, urged Wheeler to meet his buddy H. L. Mencken, who he said could "really write," and who hosted unforgettable evenings in Philadelphia at something called the Saturday Night Club. "We meet together at eight o'clock each Saturday night and play symphonies until ten. Then we drink beer, eat and converse upon sundry subjects until midnight or later. I think you will not find anywhere now in existence a more highly 'he' group than this, nor one in which Rabelaisian conversation reaches such genuinely high flights" (cited in Evans and Evans, 247).

Mencken, indeed, could write. He was an ardent fan of Nietzsche and an early proponent of the work of Ayn Rand. He was also a vicious racist, though in his private journals he noted that it was in bad taste to talk about that kind of thing in public. Presumably it was okay at his weekly salon.

I wondered if Mencken made Wheeler consider "the problem of the male," but the Evanses' biography went on: "Over the years Wheeler attended a number of meetings of the Saturday Night Club, for Wheeler greatly admired Mencken and may have been influenced by Mencken's free-swinging style and his iconoclastic views" (248). When I read this, of course, my heart sank.

Some forty pages later in the biography, there's a strange paragraph:

> Wheeler's activities for the year 1925 ... had two unexpected consequences: the discovery in Paris of an unpublished manuscript of Réaumur on ants (subsequently published), and a "slight mental breakdown," as he called it. The latter did not come at once, but in early 1926 Wheeler did not feel well, and during February and March he was at a mental hospital near New York City. In between coppersmithing and the like, however, he read [the] proof[s] of his French book, *Les Sociétés d'Insectes*. From April first through the summer he spent most of his days at Colebrook [his country home] relaxing. (286)

Despite my increasing discomfort in reading the biography, I was moved by the Evanses' discretion on this episode.

* * *

Over our picnic lunch today by an algae-covered pond, S got a dreamy look in his eyes and said, "A raw egg he would also appreciate." It took me a minute to realize he was talking about the hedgehog.

* * *

Although most of his books were highly specialized and published by academic presses, through his association with Mencken, Wheeler was invited to publish one volume of collected essays and lectures with Alfred A. Knopf. I received my copy of *Foibles of Insects and Men*, Wheeler's crossover book, before finishing the biography, and I decided to pause in my reading of *William Morton Wheeler, Biologist* to take a look at what Knopf thought might be of interest to a lay reader. The Evanses had hinted that the last essay in the volume was a humdinger, and indeed it was. But I'll get to that later. For now, I'll say that in general, I didn't actually find *Foibles* any more or less absorbing than what I'd already read. That is, the essays are mostly comprised of Wheeler's characteristic mix of detailed entomological observation, highfalutin literary references, and action-packed cross-species parables. I found all that equally compelling, but I'm not sure how well the book sold. I just checked the current Amazon ranking: number 10,173,328 in books. Hm, that made me feel a little better about the current ranking of my last novel: number 981,739. Anyway, there was one essay I thought might be of particular interest to S, a lecture originally delivered to the American Association for the Advancement of Science on the occasion of Wheeler's retirement from the chairmanship of Section F (Zoological Sciences) of that organization in 1920. The lecture was titled "The Organization of Research," but Wheeler began his paper with a "confession":

> I find myself in a somewhat unpleasant predicament, for when I began [the paper] and even after sending its title to Professor Allee I was of the opinion that research might, perhaps, be amenable to organization, but after thinking the matter over I was compelled to reverse my opinion, with the result that what I shall say may strike some of you as painfully reactionary. Still I encouraged myself with the reflection that many others have written papers with misleading titles and that I might perhaps put much of the blame for the results on my confrères of Section F for conferring so signal an honor as

its chairmanship on one of its tired old bisons from the taxonomic menagerie instead of on one of its fresh young bulls from the Mendelian byre. (169)

He goes on to disparage the trendy fixation on the term *organization*, which he notes had only recently usurped the late Victorian fascination with "progress." "The mediaeval high-brow words were 'chivalry,' and 'honor,'" which he compares to the Greek notion of *aidos* and the Japanese ideal of Bushido, the samurai code of honor. "All of these conceptions—progress, organization, chivalry, aidos, bushido—seem to start among the intellectual aristocracy and all imply a certain 'noblesse-oblige,' for there is no fun in continually exhorting others to progress unless you can keep up with the procession, or organizing others unless you yearn to be organized yourself, just as there is no fun in getting up a dueling or bushido code unless you are willing to fight duels or commit hara-kiri whenever it is required by the rules of the game" (169–70).

Wheeler's more interested in foraging, and in the work of amateurs. He derides the reverence of professionalism in the sciences and dreams of a future commonwealth in which "the communal furnace-man, after his four-hour day, is conducting elaborate investigations in paleo-botany, and … the communal laundress is an acknowledged authority in colloidal chemistry" (177–78).

I tried reading this passage out loud to S. He's a committed amateur, and he's profoundly disorganized, in the best sense of the term. He finds it befuddling that I tend to write from an outline. His experiments breeding toads and salamanders in our house have been surprisingly successful, given that his methods are entirely improvised. But as I read aloud from *Foibles*, I noticed that S had the faraway look he sometimes gets when I try to turn him on to some book or film or piece of music. I think he was probably trying to come up with some new delicacy to offer the hedgehog.

* * *

Sarah just wrote me from Athens. She said, "i've spent about a month reading everything kropotkin ever wrote, and then almost everything cedric robinson ever wrote, and then rereading them both while taking scrupulous notes." She was in a funk because of Robinson's critique of anarchism in relation to false notions of "order." But she was beginning to see a glimmer of hope in resolving the conundrum. In other news, the library is slowly taking shape. Sarah and a comrade just located a "recent divorcée who runs a bookshop," and in dividing the marital assets, this woman got custody of a thirty-year collection of Greek queer feminist zines. "she doesn't have a place to store them and we're hoping she leaves them with us!"

* * *

I have my own confession to make. Like Wheeler, and unlike my friend the gynarchivist and my anarchist student, I am not a vegetarian. I was, for many years, but when I got pregnant at the age of thirty, I found myself having irresistible cravings for meat. I figured my body was telling me what I needed, so I listened, and I never really turned back. If I try to take stock of my political flaws, I usually find that my major failing is my anthropocentrism. Of course, even if you're anthropocentric, that's not much of an excuse since a plant-based diet is beneficial for humanity as well as for other animals. But it feels to me like eating meat is part of my animal nature.

Even S, who obviously loves critters with a passion, eats them. A while ago, he rescued an injured pheasant from a cat who'd attacked it. He's been keeping the pheasant in a little coop at the back of the garden. It's a male, and it's now fully recovered, fat, with beautiful tail feathers. He thought about releasing it, but he's worried it won't survive after being domesticated. My son is coming to visit us in a couple of days, and S, though clearly ambivalent, suggested that maybe we should eat the pheasant together. I think it's a good idea. I always told my son that if you're going to eat meat, it's better to really grapple with the fact of what you're doing, and witness, if possible, the slaughter, rather than just picking up a plastic-wrapped package of chicken legs at the grocery store. S knows very well how to kill, pluck, and clean a fowl. He also likes to crunch, occasionally, on some dried ants that he brought back in a bag after a trip to Korea. He's even eaten hedgehog. He told me the Romani cook hedgehog by encasing it in clay and roasting it in hot ashes. It seems that when you break open the clay case, the quills all come out.

S's mother was from Romania, though she wasn't Romani. She was Jewish, and during the war, she and her mother were smuggled out of Cluj (then under Hungarian rule) by S's father, who was French. Most of her family was less fortunate.

* * *

As I said, there were some things I appreciated about the Evanses' biography of Wheeler, including their discretion about his mental illness. But the day I finished the book, I wanted to throw it across the room. I couldn't believe what they'd done. In the last few pages, they tried to come up with some sort of honest reckoning of his qualities, both good and bad.

> His incessant energy took its toll on his nervous system, and he had neurotic tendencies throughout his life. His diaries and letters contain many references to the state of his health, and from time to time he had periods of depression, the worst being his collapse in 1926. But, as we have shown, even in the hospital he could not completely escape his absorption in his writing.... Wheeler was an incessant smoker, preferring a pipe but sometimes using cigars or even cigarettes when he ran out of pipe tobacco. (217)

Naturally, that made me remember his quip about the maternal breast in addressing the Royce Club in 1917. It also made me think of S. He smoked for nearly fifty years, until his doctor finally convinced him, recently, to switch to an electronic cigarette. He refers to it as his *tétine,* "his pacifier."

The Evanses went on a bit about Wheeler's penchant for card playing, noting that he was "not always the best loser," and described him as a basically shy person, but one who was capable of lively storytelling, not all of it appropriate for "polite society." And then, the bombshell: "In informal gatherings he was often the center of attention, and it was here that his numerous prejudices came to the surface: geneticists, psychologists, and even Jews (whom he enjoyed citing as examples of social parasitism)" (317).

Here, there was a paragraph break. But the cracking I felt wasn't that of the paragraph. It was the breaking of my heart. I was on page 317, in a book of 319 pages.

The Evanses went on to give a sort of lame apologia that begins, "His streak of antisemitism is curious, for one of Wheeler's closest friends at the German-English Seminary and during the years immediately following was a Jewish boy named Adolph Bernhard. . . ." Wheeler had maintained a correspondence with this friend, although only Bernhard's letters survived. According to the Evanses, in their correspondence, Wheeler and Bernhard "exchanged confidences about the future of the world, thoughts on women, on professors, on being Jewish, and on other subjects common to most friends age twenty" (317–18). Needless to say, this provided little balm for my distress.

In truth, my uneasy feelings had begun long before, when I encountered that list of human parasites. "Criminals, hoboes, defectives, prostitutes, white-slavers"—all of those were obviously troubling. But I was perturbed by another term, perhaps all the more pernicious because it seemed to me a code word: *usurers*.

When I told S about this, he smiled grimly and agreed.

* * *

I know that S loves me, and he's generally very tolerant of my way of making a living, though he's resisted academicism all his life and is, as you will have surmised, a confirmed autodidact. He's also been surprised by the generosity and cordiality of many of my colleagues, whom he now counts as friends—which is especially remarkable given his constitutional solitary ways. But when I regale him with stories of departmental politics, he can't help expressing bewilderment. Or maybe detachment is the word. Sometimes I feel defensive, but mostly I think he's right.

Despite his lengthy and celebrated career as a professor, William Morton Wheeler was also pretty grumpy about academicism. The penultimate essay in *Foibles of Insects and Men* is a rant addressed to the American Society of Naturalists in 1923. It's called "The Dry-Rot of Our Academic Biology." It opens with a series of scathing epigraphs—among them, Schiller citing William James: *"The natural enemy of any subject is the professor thereof!"* (188). Wheeler then begins his paper by apologizing for his state of exhaustion, saying he's just "laid" a volume of 1,100 pages on ants. "This racking oviposition leaves me reduced to a mere blob of *corpora lutea* and so feeble that I can only crawl. . . ." (189). Still, he manages to attain an astonishing pitch of vituperation, skewering his colleagues for feeding their students with "pedagogical pabulum." He elaborates:

> To us gerontic schoolmarms in trousers, who have flown from reality and have slowly succumbed to autistic thinking, with defective eyesight, doughy musculature, brittle ossifications, demoralized intestines, decayed autonomic nervous systems, and atrophied interstitials, there comes every year a small army of freshmen—very properly so called—in their late teens and early twenties, burning for impact with reality, with exquisite sense-organs, superb bones, muscles and alimentary tracts, mirific endocrine and autonomic apparatus, and a mentality of nine to fourteen years or thereabouts—and what do we give them? (196–97)

Dry rot. That's what we do with the freshmen. As for our graduate students, we try to turn them "into mere vehicles of our own interests" (197). I had a moment of self-consciousness reading that but then assuaged myself a little by remembering that it's usually my graduate students who turn me on to things, like Sarah and her anarchist, bee-loving friend.

At the end of his address, Wheeler makes another a plea for amateurism and ends up sounding like he wished he'd carried out his career here in the garden in Pourry rather than hunkering down in the classrooms of Harvard.

> It quite saddens me to think that when I cross the Styx, I may find myself among so many professional biologists, condemned to keep on trying to solve problems, and that Pluto, or whoever is in charge down there now, may condemn me to sit forever trying to identify specimens from my own specific and generic diagnoses, while the amateur entomologists, who have not been damned professors, are permitted to roam at will among the fragrant asphodels of the Elysian meadows, netting gorgeous, ghostly butterflies until the end of time. (204)

* * *

In some floundering attempt to recover from those last pages of the biography, I did something perhaps as useless as the Evanses' "some of his best friends were Jews." I went back to look at more of his essays on parasitism, hoping maybe to find some redeeming flip-flopping Wheelerism. I know, I know. But for what it's worth.

"Insect Parasitism and Its Peculiarities" has two epigraphs. The first, from Emerson (Ralph Waldo, not Dora, nor her father, Ralph E.): "Whoever looks at the insect world, at flies, aphids, gnats and innumerable parasites, and even at the infant mammals, must have remarked the extreme content they take in suction, which constitutes the main business of their life. If we go into a library or news-room, we see the same function on a higher plane, performed with like ardor, with equal impatience of interruption, indicating the sweetness of the act" (47).

I liked that image of sucking up written language. S and I begin each day with a half hour or so of this kind of activity over coffee. He's currently deep into Wilhelm Bölsche, whom he discovered through Ferenczi. I don't need to tell you what I've been slurping on.

Wheeler's second epigraph is from J. H. Fabre's *Souvenirs Entomologiques*, volume 3, in which he finds man *"le grand parasite,"* today the eater, tomorrow the eaten. Early in his paper, Wheeler illustrates the phenomenon of human parasitism in a compressed little life story:

> As an embryo he is always entoparasitic, using his allantois in a manner that vividly suggests the root-system of a Sacculina attached to a crab. At birth he becomes a kind of ectoparasite on his mother or nurse, and throughout his childhood and youth he is commonly what might be called a family parasite, depending for his sustenance on his parents, brothers and sisters or remoter relations. At maturity, in addition to the possibility of becoming parasitic on his wife, he has a choice of many kinds of social parasitism. As a member of a trust, political party or legislative body, not to mention many other organizations and institutions [obviously including universities], he may graft successfully on the community at large or on some particularly lucrative portion of it, and should he fail through these activ-

ities to store up a sufficient *corpus adiposum* in the form of a bank-account, he may parasitize, with advancing years and till the end of his days, on his own offspring. (47)

It's interesting that Wheeler's exemplary human parasite is a boy. I would never call my son "parasitic," although he did breastfeed for nearly three years. But that may have had as much to do with my enthusiasm about breastfeeding as it did with his appetite for it. I also loved being pregnant.

My mother, like me, raised her children on her own, and she always encouraged us to be independent. She said: "I'll help pay for your education, but once you turn twenty-one, you're on your own. Don't come asking for money. And by the same token, I'm saving up for my old age so I'll never have to come knocking on your door." It's true, she managed to squirrel enough away so she could pay for her own nursing home, though of course my sister and I gladly would have helped if she'd needed it. It was only when I had my own child that I realized that her policy on family money was a little extreme. Still, I must have passed something of this on to my son, as he takes a great deal of pride in his independence.

The bulk of the rest of Wheeler's essay is a detailed account of various entomological parasitic and para-parasitic tendencies such as hypermetamorphosis among the Proctotrypids, Chalcidids, Hymenoptera, Mantispa, Strepsiptera, and Coleoptera; hyperparasitism among the caterpillars; and viviparity among the larviparous Tachinidae and Sarcophagidae, the nymphiparous Hippoboscidae, Nycteribidae, and plant lice. It's hard to believe Knopf took this on. Mencken must have pulled a lot of strings.

My son arrived yesterday. Over the past few weeks, he's been traveling around Europe taking photographs, and he scheduled this visit in between Paris and Amsterdam. He seems enchanted by the little camp site we fixed up for him next to the forest. Today at lunch, S asked us if we thought it was time to bump off the pheasant. It seems it's best to let the meat rest for a day or two before cooking it, and Leo's only here for two more nights. Leo seemed curious, and, as I said, I approved of the plan. But you could see in S's demeanor that he was nervous about it. He told Leo that in his youth he'd shared his father's "hunter spirit" and had trapped and shot all manner of game. He'd also spent a period in the Arctic, and he much admired the Inuit approach to wildlife, which was simultaneously reverential and highly utilitarian. They use every part of the seal they hunt. But he also told us that, after all these years, he found it harder and harder to deal with the moment of slaughter. Maybe he'd just seen enough death.

I said I'd offer to do it myself, but having no experience, I worried I'd cause the pheasant unnecessary pain if I bungled things. Leo pulled out his phone to look up a YouTube video on "humane slaughter of chickens." He asked, "Do you have an axe?" S shook his head at our clearly naive attempts to be of use. He marched over to the coop with resignation. Leo held the bird by the legs while S whacked it on the head with a big stick. It was over in seconds.

The pheasant flapped for a bit, and then its eyes closed. It was so beautiful. Leo and I stayed with it for a while in silence, just holding our hands on its warm, quiet body. It took us a while to realize that S had left. He was taking a walk, alone. He'd found that very difficult.

* * *

I've been holding off on telling you about the last essay in *Foibles of Insects and Men*. It's called "The Termitodoxa, or Biology and Society." It's held by many to be Wheeler's most fanciful, indeed eccentric, piece of writing. In it, he claims to have been inspired by recent tales of animal intelligence, such as the "Elberfield stallions" who, just before World War I, were reportedly trained to solve arithmetic problems, read, spell, and answer basic questions. (Unfortunately, they were conscripted as "draft horses" during the war and disappeared.) Wheeler says that based on these stories, he decided to attempt some "animal correspondence." Worried about the flood of mail he might receive if he tried too many species, he opted to "proceed with caution and confine myself at first to a single letter to the most wonderful of all insects, the queen of the West African *Termes bellicosus.*" A purported missionary friend offered to serve as the intermediary but reminded Wheeler that, unlike his beloved ants, the termites had a king as well as a queen, though "the *bellicosus* king was so accustomed to being overlooked, even by his own offspring, that he not only pardoned my discourtesy but condescended to answer my letter" (207).

The rest of the essay is entirely, or nearly entirely, comprised of the letter from the king, who begins by explaining why he's answering a missive that had been addressed to the queen. "Her majesty, being extremely busy with oviposition—she has laid an egg every three minutes for the past four years—and fearing that an interruption of even twenty minutes might seriously upset the exquisitely balanced routine of the termitarium," has requested that the king handle Wheeler's queries, which were evidently based on some "anxiety" regarding the comparative social blundering of his own species (207–8).

The king presents himself as an avid student of termite society. "As you know, the conditions under which I live are most conducive to sustained research. I am carefully fed, have all the leisure in the world, and the royal chamber is not only kept absolutely dark and at a constant and agreeable temperature even during the hottest days of the Ethiopian summer, but free from all noises except the gentle rhythmic dropping of her majesty's eggs and the soft footfalls of the workers on the cement floor as they carry away the germs of future populations to the royal nurseries." The king also claims some familiarity with Wheeler's society, having belonged in his youth to a colony that "devoured and digested a well-selected library" belonging to a bookish missionary. He hesitates to recommend that Wheeler's species strictly follow the termites' example but imagines his observations may be of interest, since "you and your fellow human beings are after all only animals like myself" (208–9).

The letter covers traditions developed since the time of the ancestors in early Cretaceous times. They hit a snag in the middle of the Cretaceous Period, when rampant reproduction was accompanied by social degeneration.

> The priests, pedagogues, politicians and journalists having bored their way up to the highest stratum of the society undertook to influence or control all the activities of its members.

The priests tried to convince the people that if they would only give up indulging in the social hormones and confine themselves to a diet of pure mud, they would in a future life eat nothing but rose-wood and mahogany, and the pedagogues insisted that every young termite must thoroughly saturate himself with the culture and languages of the Upper Carboniferous cockroaches.... The politicians and the journalists— well, were it not that profanity has been considered to be very bad form in termite society since the Miocene, I might make a few comments on *their* activities.... Meanwhile in the very foundations of the commonwealth anarchists, syndicalists, iww and bolsheviki were busy boring holes and filling them with dynamite, while the remainder of society was largely composed of profiteers, grafters, shysters, drug-fiends and criminals of all sizes interspersed with beautifully graduated series of wowsers, morons, feeble-minded, idiots and insane. (210)

"Wowsers," the king explains in a note, is a term invented by Australian termites, later taken up by humans of that region, to refer to what we might call bozos. He praises the intervention of his predecessor, King Wuf-wuf IV, of the 529th dynasty, who initiated a series of social reforms, displaying "the statesmanship of a Hammurabi, Moses, Solomon, Solon and Pericles rolled into one." In his "moments of relaxation he was a delightful blend of Aristophanes, Lucian, Rabelais, Anatole France and Bernard Shaw." Fortunately, termite society was "ambisexual throughout, so that, unlike the ants, we have male as well as female soldiers and workers." They took in certain beetles and flies, caring for them "till they developed exudate organs" that spiced up the hormonal situation in the colonies. But they had to limit the numbers of these rousing guests "for the same reason that your society would find it advisable to restrict the cattle industry if your animal breeders had succeeded in producing breeds of cows that yielded highballs and cocktails instead of milk" (210–12).

There was another social reform, a "very effective method of dealing with any termite that attempted to depart from the standards of the most perfect social behavior." Basically, the culprit's usefulness was reduced to "the amount of fat and proteins in his constitution. He was then led forth into the general assembly, dismembered and devoured by his fellows." The king realizes that this system might seem harsh from Wheeler's perspective, but he makes a case for it: "To the perfectly socialized termite nothing can be more blissful or exalted than feeling the precious fats and proteins which he has amassed with so much labor, melting, without the slightest loss of their vital values, into the constitutions of his more vigorous and socially more efficient fellow beings" (211–12). Needless to say, this applies not only to social deviants but also to those who are declining with age.

He finds human attempts to form classes "purely superficial," with only three "spurious castes" in operation:

The young, the mature and the aged. These, of course, resemble our castes only in number and in consisting of individuals of both sexes. They are peculiar in being rather poorly defined, temporary portions of the life-cycle, so that a single individual may belong to all of them in succession, and in the fact that only one of them, comprising the mature individuals, is of any great economic value to society and therefore actually functions as the host of the two others, which are, biologically speaking, parasitic. To avoid shocking your human sensibilities, I am willing to admit that both these castes may be worth all the care that is bestowed on them, the young on account of their promise and the old on account of past services. (215)

But, he continues, he finds it perplexing that our species coddles the elderly to the extent that we do, allowing them to maintain positions of authority—even those who "combine with a surprising physical vigor a certain sadistic obstinacy" that gets in the way of any social advancement. The king recommends, in such cases, the administration of chloroform, or maybe even "some more vigorous insecticide, such as hydrocyanic acid gas." He signs his letter, "Yours truly, Wee-Wee, 43rd Neotenic King, of the 8,429th Dynasty of the Bellicose Termites" (215–17).

Wheeler closes his lecture:

On reperusing this letter before deciding, after many misgivings, to read it to so serious a body of naturalists, I notice a great number of inaccuracies and exaggerations, attributable, no doubt, to his majesty's misinterpretation of his own and very superficial acquaintance with our society. His remarks on old age strike me as particularly inept and offensive. He seems not to be aware of the fact that at least a few of our old men have almost attained to the idealism of the superannuated termite, a fact attested by such Freudian confessions as the following, taken from a letter recently received by one of my colleagues from a gentleman in New Hampshire:

I do not understand how it is that an insect so small as to be invisible is able to worry my dog and also at times sharply to bite myself. A vet. friend of mine in Boston advised lard and kerosene for the dog. This seemed to check them for a time, but what I need is extermination, for I am in my eighty-fourth year. (217)

the mother of forensic science

....

A couple of years ago, the Renwick Gallery at the Smithsonian Institution mounted an exhibit of the *Nutshell Studies of Unexplained Death*—a series of miniature sculptural works created in the mid-twentieth century by Frances Glessner Lee. The exhibit displayed Lee's original pieces, and the museum's website posted some beautiful photographic images of them. But the curators of the exhibit were adamant about something: two-dimensional photographs can't possibly convey the complexity of the nutshells, which they likened to the contemporary medium we call "virtual reality." In fact, they tried to use that medium on the Smithsonian website, giving you the opportunity to "explore" some of the rooms from within. But, needless to say, even that technology can't approximate what sticking your head or your fingers in there would. Still, I'll reproduce a couple of images here, first of Lee herself and then of her *Nutshell Studies*, which were accompanied by the Smithsonian's brief biography of Lee and the curators' gloss on her significance to both forensic and art history:

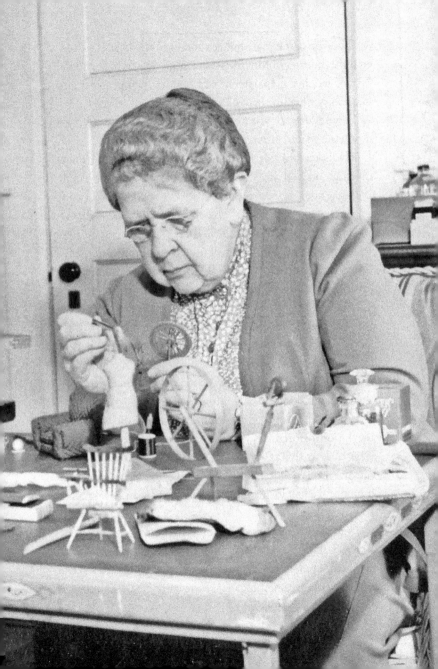

"Lee, the first female police captain in the U.S., is considered the 'mother of forensic science' and helped to found the first-of-its kind Department of Legal Medicine at Harvard University when the field of forensics was in its infancy."

I pause here to point out the interesting figures of both motherhood and infancy in defining Lee's significance.

The biography goes on to note that in the 1940s, criminal investigators had little training in how to examine or handle evidence at crime scenes, and it was Lee's artistic practice as a miniaturist—a practice she'd begun in childhood—that allowed her to re-create crime scenes with such accuracy.

In fact, the nutshells are still used for training purposes at the Office of the Chief Medical Examiner in Baltimore. "Every element of the dioramas—from the angle of minuscule bullet holes, the placement of latches on widows, the patterns of blood splatters, and the discoloration of painstakingly painted miniature corpses—challenges trainees' powers of observation and deduction." The point is that the miniature crime scenes teach people how to look at evidence: carefully, slowly, painstakingly, and in three dimensions.

But to me, the most extraordinary thing Lee did was not to revolutionize forensic science—it was to knit the socks of her victims. I say this as a miniaturist and as a knitter. Socks are fucking hard to knit, even if the foot you're making them for is nine and a half inches long. Did she do this on sewing pins? I am utterly abashed.

It wasn't my mother who taught me to knit. Though she was very crafty, for some reason knitting was a skill she never acquired. I taught myself how to do it as an adult around the time it became something of a cliché among a certain kind of

fig 2.2 Nutshell (Smithsonian)

fig 2.3 Socks (Smithsonian)

femme feminists (surely you remember the "stitch 'n' bitch" craze of the early aughts). Among the traditional fiber arts, my mother favored crewel embroidery, but she occasionally embarked on more quirky projects, like a pint-sized couple of naked elderly stuffed dolls, the man with a paunch and a sagging penis, the woman with droopy dugs. She could be playful but she was also a realist.

My mother died on January 23, 2019, after a few strokes and several years of both cognitive and physical difficulties. They were treating her for these, but it came to the point that the treatments for one condition would increase the risks of another, and she was experiencing side effects from everything. Finally, the doctors recommended just giving her some morphine and letting nature take its course, which it did, quickly. When her GP came into her room and gently told her, "Elinor, you're dying," she said, "Thank God." She meant that figuratively. She didn't believe in God.

Smoker, realist, atheist, lady, democratic socialist, pragmatist. My mother was also a feminist. Perhaps this goes without saying, but I'll say it: it's the womanly—in fact, the girlish—art of dollhouse "play" that allowed Frances Glessner Lee to see things that other people couldn't, or hadn't, or wouldn't, and to solve certain crimes, in particular those against working-class women that preoccupied her most. Those things preoccupied my mother as well.

* * *

Sarah, my anarcha-feminist student and friend, sent me an email saying she'd read about a book I might like on somebody's blogpost. It was *LaBrava* by Elmore Leonard, the eminent crime novelist. I ordered a used copy and tore right through it. The titular character is a young photographer who accidentally gets caught up in a Miami Beach scam. It opens with a description of his art photographs, which sounded uncannily like those my son takes—and in fact, the character resembled my son in many ways. There's another character—a fading former movie star who can't quite distinguish between her movie roles and her life—who bore a weird resemblance to me (this is why Sarah thought I might be intrigued). As I was beginning my reading of this novel, I texted my son in a fit of enthusiasm and told him I was reading a crime novel starring the two of us. Then I read on and became deeply embarrassed when the young photographer and the middle-aged former actress went to bed together, even though she was almost old enough to be his mother.

I quickly texted him again and told him to forget the comparison, but I kept reading *LaBrava*. And, in fact, it started me thinking that Leo might, in fact, be interested in forensic photography as a professional sideline. When I told him that, he thought it sounded like something to look into. Of course, when we both researched this possibility, we saw that this kind of work is often done by actual cops, which was not what either of us had in mind, but perhaps because of all this thinking I'd been doing about Frances Glessner Lee's higher motives (paying attention to the violences perpetrated against the most vulnerable and disregarded of people), forensic science had a certain appeal. Also, now that practically everybody considers him or herself a photographer, the promise of remuneration for art photography seems increasingly remote.

I also thought of Frances Glessner Lee when I read that book by my other friend, the one I called a "gynarchivist." Her name is Julietta Singh, and her book begins with a crime scene. The heat's gone out again in young Julietta's studio apartment, and she's padding around in woolly socks (presumably of normal size), wondering if an intruder lurks outside her door. There's a robber that's been hitting her building recently, but up to now, her place has been spared. He did, however, take her sneakers, which she'd left outside the door. In an effort to take control of the situation, she finds a can of Red Bull that somebody left behind at her place—an item she neither values nor wants. She sticks a yellow Post-it Note on the can that reads, something like the bottle in Alice in Wonderland, "Please Feel Free." She puts it in the fridge. "Waiting to be robbed," Julietta writes, "is like waiting for an imminent accident in which both you and your assailant are together in disaster" (17). I found that a very beautiful line. Who are we when we place ourselves inside that nutshell? What's our complicity in the crime? I decided to make a tiny crime scene, to see if it could help me answer the question. I got out some tiny scissors, tweezers, and glue.

Once I got started, I couldn't seem to stop. I must confess, I availed myself of some technologies that Frances Glessner Lee didn't have—in particular, my computer, where I snagged a JPEG of a Red Bull label off the internet and shrunk it down to one twelfth of its regular size and then hit "print." I also purchased a 1:12 dollhouse refrigerator on Etsy. But I did rummage up a perfectly proportioned little canister-shaped piece of metal, trimmed the Red Bull label with great accuracy, and

fig 2.4 Red Bull (B. Browning)

glued it onto the can. I found the canister in a kitchen drawer in which I keep all manner of useless objects. I have no idea where it came from or what its original purpose was. That drawer in my kitchen is a mess. Up until she started having those cognitive difficulties, my mother was a meticulous housekeeper. Her own kitchen drawers were very organized.

* * *

How could one craft the "nutshells" that Julietta calls "the vaginal archive"? As I said, that's the term that first made me want to call her a "gynarchivist." In forensic terms, the crime, in the eyes of the Argentine dictatorship, was holding a subversive text in one's internal cells. The crime of the dictatorship, to our

fig 2.5 Karl Marx and Organic Produce (B. Browning)

eyes, was holding those women in prison cells. I told myself: it's a nutshell in a nutshell. If we place ourselves there, with care, maybe we can begin to read, really read, the tiny writing hidden there. One of the images of Frances Glessner Lee's work includes a mound of personal correspondence, apparently penned by hand. It's not possible to read the contents of the letters in the photograph. I'm not sure if you could read them up close and personal, with a magnifying glass. I also don't know if Frances Glessner Lee actually reproduced the letters found at the scene of the crime or if she fictionalized them.

There's another crime scene, quite literal, depicted in Julietta's book: a mugging she experienced as a student during her first extended stay in the United States (Julietta is Canadian by birth).

She lists the items she was carrying: a set of keys for her new apartment, her ID, a paperback version of *The Communist Manifesto,* a DVD of *Sense and Sensibility,* and some organic produce from a health food store. It was the DVD that was her "downfall." She'd dawdled in the video store, a little embarrassed to be checking out a Victorian romance. By the time she left the store, it was getting dark, and four boys approached her with a machete. I won't take you through the harrowing part, though in fact she narrates it with relative sangfroid. They were boys, in fact, probably just as scared as she was. As they run off, the smallest of the boys, in an effort to prove himself, bolts back to snatch the fallen vegetables. She says, "'Really?! You're going to jump a girl *and* steal her groceries?!' . . . just before he rounded a corner to vanish forever, he turned back to me and hollered so sweetly and sincerely, 'I'm sorry, ma'am!'" (107).

Julietta says that in her memory of that crime scene, "there are only objects and words, words as objects" (107). But they're crafted with care, like Frances Glessner Lee's little socks. It's in that writerly crafting that we see why the fine art of forensics, in all of its delicacy, is so necessary. By "crafting," of course, I'm referring to Julietta's scripting of that scene and also to the care with which she places herself in it, as another object among objects, all circumscribed by circumstances.

Again, I confess to having procured the miniature organic produce on Etsy, and to having printed out the tiny JPEGs of the covers of *The Communist Manifesto* and *Sense and Sensibil-*

ity. I did, however, hand-cut the keys out of some brass-colored metallic paper I also found in that chaotic kitchen drawer.

* * *

I went through a period of knitting socks—normal-sized socks—but as I said, they're tricky to make, and eventually I stopped. I make plenty of baby booties and other little garments for friends and students who are expecting. Over the years, I've made a few fingerless gloves for my son and other smaller items for people I love. Some for people I barely know. S asked me if I could knit him a replica of Paul McCartney's famous argyle vest, and I gamely ordered the fine skeins of multicolored wool, but I'm not sure when I'll ever get around to it. That would take a lot of time, and concentration. I like tiny projects. When S gave up smoking and switched to an e-cigarette, I made him a couple of little e-cigarette holders to wear around his neck. Back in the "pussy hat" period, I made a few of those, even though I understood the reservations of some of my friends to the fad: the color pink (too femme, too white) and the ostensible gender essentialism. The counter-argument to the first objection might also sound a little too bio-literalistic: everybody has pink parts. I tried to mitigate the second objection by crafting a couple of miniature pussy hats just big enough for somebody to wear on the head of their penis. They were, if I say so myself, fairly adorable.

I was sort of hoping they might go viral, but they didn't. I didn't show those to my mother, as I thought they might confuse her. After her strokes, she found a lot of things more confusing. But obviously, this impulse was somehow related to her own slightly obscene little craft projects.

fig 2.6 Pussy Hats (B. Browning)

fig 2.7 *The Audacity of Hope*
(African American Miniature Museum)

This, along with my shortcuts on the Julietta miniatures, may make me look less meticulous in my craftsmanship than I should be. I felt a little less embarrassed about using my computer to shrink *The Communist Manifesto* when I saw a photograph of an obviously shrunken copy of Barack Obama's *The Audacity of Hope* on a tiny chair arranged by Karen Collins.

It was highly pixilated, though Collins seemed to have done an excellent job of affixing the cover to a diminutive perfect bound dummy of the book itself. *Perfect bound* is a bookmaking term: it's the cheapest and easiest way to make a paperback, gluing the pages together along the spine. Collins acknowledges that her miniatures aren't actually perfect. But that doesn't mean they're not made with care.

Karen Collins is about S's age. She was born in Compton, California, and raised by a single mom. She says she didn't have a dollhouse as a girl because they were too expensive, but she managed to make her own out of cardboard boxes. As a teenager, she was active in the civil rights movement. In the '70s, she married Ed Lewis, and they had two children. Her son, Eddie, was born in 1974. In a video documentary, Collins says, "I thought nobody ever loved anybody as much as I loved my son." I'm sure she also loves her daughter. Anyway, Collins wasn't just a devoted mother to her two children. She also worked in a preschool. She says she bought her first dollhouse when she was forty, and she started decorating it—not just with little midcentury furniture, but also with figurines she'd craft by hand. According to an article published a few years ago in the *Los Angeles Times*: "To make it look like a black family lived inside, she built little picture frames with black faces and hung them on the wallpapered walls. She made itsy-bitsy versions of black magazines and glued them to the coffee tables. She sculpted tiny food out of clay and wood for the kitchen—collard greens, glazed ham and black-eyed peas." She told that reporter that when she started making those miniature scenes, "Everything was whimsical and happy" (Bermudez).

In 1991, a few weeks before his high school graduation, her son was arrested. He was driving a car, and a passenger shot at somebody. It was, everyone agrees, gang related. The charges were attempted murder and discharging a firearm from a moving vehicle. Eddie had been arrested twice before, so he was subject to the "three strikes" sentencing laws. They gave him 167 years in prison.

Karen Collins says that after her son was convicted, she became very depressed. She kept asking herself what she might have done differently as a mother to keep him out of trouble. She said she didn't feel like eating or even bathing. She quit her job. The only thing she knew how to do was make miniatures, but now they weren't so whimsical. She began thinking of them as political. She started thinking they might be educational, and inspirational. She made little figures of Harriet Tubman and Thurgood Marshall, Malcolm X and Martin Luther King Jr.

More recently, she's made dioramas of Black Lives Matter protests. She says she doesn't go out and march herself—she stays home and makes miniatures. She has a website with pictures of her dioramas. She wants to put them in a permanent

fig 2.8 I Can't Breathe
(African American Miniature Museum)

museum space—in fact, there's a diorama with a miniature fictional museum of African American miniatures. A nutshell in a nutshell. Right now, all her work is stored in her house, but she takes her pieces to libraries and schools.

It's Collins's husband who makes the boxes that contain her miniatures. He appears to be a very gentle and supportive husband. Collins credits him with the design feature of a glass top, "so the light could get in." She says, "He always wanted my success." She says that he can whip off a box in no time at all—"It's me that takes time." I guess he'd build something bigger for her if he could. Karen Collins says:

> In my mind, in the future, we have a building that we can use and renovate, where we still have the museum expanded, and

that I might have a creative room to work with children and teach them how to accomplish this craft, maybe have a little library for children in there…. [Her imaginary permanent museum is] a happy place, it's a safe place for families to spend time. Because this is not a looky-loo where you can just look at it and go. You have to spend some time with your child so they will know the truth. (African American Miniature Museum)

Karen Collins, of course, may be a dreamer, but she's also a mother of forensic science.

* * *

After I made my own miniatures of Julietta's crime scenes, I gave them to her. I wanted her to know that I'd been reading her book carefully. Later she told me that when she brought the little objects home, they were quickly appropriated by her daughter, who began making her own miniature things.

dilation and contraction

....

or a few weeks after my mother died, I wondered, as I had on a couple of other occasions in my life, if the numbness I was feeling would ever lift. Each time this happened, I knew it would, but it was hard to imagine. It wasn't pain so much as a feeling of floating. One day I went to the department to teach a seminar and came home to find a beautiful bouquet of sunflowers and daisies with a note from Yve and Sarah. Yve is an artist and a dear friend of mine. Sarah is his girlfriend (and the same beloved student who turned me on to anarcha-feminist beekeeping and Elmore Leonard). They'd only just learned about what had happened through an exchange of texts I'd had with Yve. My mother's passing was long anticipated, and I didn't feel the need to notify a lot of people. In fact, I hadn't even told Yve about it at first because he was going through an extremely difficult period himself, but since he seemed to be stabilizing, I went ahead and mentioned it. He and Sarah immediately sent that bouquet. I wrote to Yve, "I arrived at my house after class to find some SUCH BEAUTIFUL FLOWERS from you two, all golden and blooming, my mother's favorite color! And then it started snowing like crazy and S and I went out and walked in the blizzard, which only lasted for a few minutes, but it was bracing and great, and I suddenly realized that for the first time since she died I was feeling a little joy." That was true. Then I wrote: "The other thing waiting for me was my purple bathing suit. I'm going to put leopard spots on it now. If you are in a condition to teach your class tomorrow I will be delighted, and I will save the leopard-spotted bathing suit for my visit to you, whenever you want that to happen, and I may wear it around our apartment for S's pleasure. But if you don't feel up to teaching tomorrow, I have everything I need to fill in for you again. I love you."

Yve was, at the time, recovering from a botched surgical procedure for Crohn's disease—a bowel resection that had gone awry, leading to a second, massive emergency operation. They'd had to open him up from his sternum down to his groin. He'd scheduled the first surgery thinking that he'd be back on his feet by the beginning of the spring semester, but given the complications, he couldn't be there for his first class, which he was teaching as an adjunct. I'd offered to take his place that first week, which happened to be just after my mother's passing. Mostly I wanted to be of help, but I also thought it might help me feel more grounded.

I was a little nervous about teaching for Yve because I'd never taught a practicum on performance art before. In my teaching, I tend to present myself as a scholar rather than a practitioner. The first week had gone well enough, I think. I'd asked Yve what he would normally do in the first class meeting, and I tried to do it—at least the introductory part, where he would have asked them to write down on index cards the way they wanted to be addressed (their preferred names, not necessarily the official ones on the class roster), their preferred pronouns, their email addresses, and anything else they thought that Yve should know about them. Then I told them that I was acting as Yve's surrogate, and I told them a little bit—well, actually, I told them a lot—about Yve's use of surrogacy in his own artistic practice. And then I asked them to act as surrogates for each other and to use the index cards, which they swapped in pairs, to introduce themselves as each other. They could redact anything they wanted to before making the swap. I told them to ask permission of each other regarding what could be read out loud and to say whether they were open to having their surrogates fictionalize something about the information they'd been given. That was because Yve and I sometimes talk about what he wants for me to fictionalize about him. When there was fictionalization among his students in that first class, we talked about what felt either disconcerting or exciting about that. People seemed to be more disconcerted by getting new names than by gender changes. Later I gave the index cards to Yve, and I told him about what had happened.

The following week, it wasn't clear whether he'd be feeling well enough to go to class, so I said I was on call if he needed me. He told me that for the second week he'd planned to have them do an in-class exercise: to craft very short "performances of contraction." In preparation for possibly teaching this class, I tried to think of what my own "performance of contraction" might be. Partly to take up time (it was a four-hour seminar), and partly because it's so great, I thought that after they'd shared their own performances, maybe I'd turn out the lights and screen the film *The Incredible Shrinking Man*, which I'd recently watched at S's urging. While it was playing, I thought I'd discreetly sneak out, leaving in my place a tiny replica of myself. The easiest option was to get a Barbie doll. I don't exactly look like a Barbie, but I have long brown hair and fairly regular features. I thought if I made the Barbie an outfit to match my own, they'd get the picture. I went to Kmart and bought the most basic model. She was wearing a very ugly painted-on lavender one-piece bathing suit with multicolor leopard spots. But when I got her home, I felt too lazy to try to replicate miniature versions of my own garments. I thought it might be easier for me to replicate a big version of her ugly bathing suit. I realized the students might be mystified by my sitting through most of class—in January no less—dressed in an ugly one-piece bathing suit, but they were, after all, aspiring performance artists, so maybe they wouldn't bat an eyelash. I ordered a lavender suit online, had it shipped overnight, and covered it with the appropriate spots in fabric paint.

Obviously, this ridiculous practical overpreparation was a way for me to convince myself that I had something to give the aspiring performance artists. It was also a way for me to distract myself from worrying about Yve and thinking about my mother.

* * *

Yve ended up teaching his own class that week. It was probably a bad idea, but he's stubborn and a little masochistic. He texted me afterward to say that he'd attempted to demonstrate for them a Martha Graham contraction, and it really hurt because his abdominal muscles had been sectioned so recently. I wrote back, "Yes, I was thinking about Graham. I'd told S you'd assigned 'contraction' pieces and he thought of labor and childbirth, also interesting. Later I tell you Berlant and Stewart's ideas about dilation. But now you should rest!"

There's a lot to say about Martha Graham's ideas about contraction and release, respectively. She often articulated them in relation to anatomy, and she insisted that the former should initiate in the pelvis—or, more specifically, she urged her students to "move from the vagina." It's been suggested that this led one of her male students to develop "vagina envy" ("Graham technique"). This was of course a reference to Sigmund Freud's notion of penis envy though, as I like to point out to my students, Freud elsewhere refers to the clitoris as "the *real* small penis" ("Fetishism," 157). I don't know if Yve went into the gendering implications of Graham technique, but it seems to me they might be significant in relation to Yve's transness.

I could go on and on about "the *real* small penis," and I often do, but right now I'm restraining myself.

Perhaps I should explain the reference I made to Lauren Berlant and Kathleen Stewart's notion of dilation. It's from a collaborative book they wrote, a collection of what might be construed as prose poems or might be condensed, lyrical critical essays. They're all written in multiples of one hundred words, and they're all citational, in the sense that each one ends by acknowledging the texts or writers or artists, or sometimes the things, that led to this response. But rather than "citations," they call these references to their sources "dilations." When Lauren showed me the manuscript of the book, I wrote back:

It seemed to me that if I were to index my own experience of reading this text, it would indicate the moments in which I felt a certain kind of "dilation" in reading, and I would want both to locate, organically, and measure that experience:

dilation, cervical, p. 11 (8 cm), pp. 20–22 (10 cm), p. 57 (6 cm); pupillary, p. 15 (7 mm), p. 29 (5 mm), p. 33 (6 mm), p. 47 (8 mm)…

That is, some of the entries let in more light and colors, and some of them make you want to push.

If you have the book, I should remind you that I was referring to the manuscript, so those page numbers may not correspond to your print version. But you get the idea. Some passages really made me feel like I'd taken shrooms. I can't say that others made me feel like I was going into labor, but it is true that they made me feel like I needed to push something out. Not a baby, of course, but language, or something. When I wrote that, I had to stop and look up what the measurements were of typical phases in the dilation of either the pupils or the cervix.

* * *

The surgery that Yve had undergone involved the construction of a temporary ileostomy, which would be reversed after his small intestine had healed. Weeks later, despite his gradual recovery, he was still getting used to the ileostomy, which, he told me in a text, was "weird." I wrote back, "Bodies are weird. Did I tell you I watched 'Fantastic Voyage' recently? :O … Raquel Welch gets slimed by antibodies. I'm just getting over a bad cold, and I keep seeing my virus as a tiny Raquel Welch that I'm smothering with goo." As I reread my text, I wonder about the wisdom of comparing my cold-related slime with Yve's much more serious health issues. It seems a little insensitive. As you can see, I'd gotten on a roll after watching *The Incredible Shrinking Man* (1957, dir. Jack Arnold). I also watched *Nain et géant* (1901, dir. George Méliès), *Amour de poche* (1957, dir. Pierre Kast, and starring—improbably—Jean Marais), *The Mysterious Island* (1961, dir. Cy Endfield), as I just said, *Fantastic Voyage* (1966, dir. Richard Fleischer), *Willy Wonka and the Chocolate Factory* (1971, dir. Mel Stuart), *The Incredible Shrinking Woman* (1981, dir. Joel Schumacher, starring Lily Tomlin!), *Honey, I Shrunk the Kids* (1989, dir. Joe Johnston, Randal Kleiser, and Dean Cundey), and *Downsizing* (2017, dir. Alexander Payne). All of these are films with what I guess you could call "performances of contraction." Well, in some of them, like *Nain et géant* and *The Mysterious Island,* the seemingly tiny people only appear so in contrast to the enormous people or creatures or objects with whom or which they're juxtaposed. I'm speaking narratively of course because that's precisely the technique used in all these films.

It was Méliès who started this experiment of depicting extra-small and extra-large people, and in *Nain et géant* it's basically just a visual joke. The film's only a minute long. In it, Méliès walks through an arched doorway, looks both ways suspiciously, and then doffs the sheet he's inexplicably got wrapped around him, as well as a hat, revealing a bald pate and a fancy set of breeches. Through a double exposure, he splits himself in two, and the figure on the left side of the screen shrinks a little, while the one on the right appears to grow to a giant stature by pulling on the top of his own head. Méliès effected this transformation by rigging the camera to a pulley system, zooming in on the right and out on the left. After briefly tormenting his smaller self, the larger self returns to his original size. The two figures thumb their noses at each other and then rejoin into one. You could probably come up with a psychoanalytic reading of this, but it was really just Méliès horsing around with the prestidigitational possibilities of double exposure.

Maya Deren experimented in a less comical way with what might also appear to be cheesy tricks—slow motion and disjunctive cuts—in order to ask questions about how film might expand both our physical and our psychic capacities. She felt cinematic manipulation could extend, for example, a dancer's technique. She also thought it could mimic, or even enact, something like a trance state. That's funny, I just made the connection between a trance state and a trans state—which maybe you could say was something Martha Graham was implicitly asking her male dancers to develop through her dance technique. I think "Move from the vagina" was something she said to her female dancers, but it seems like at least one man wanted to feel that. The most celebrated reenactor of Martha Graham's solo dances is Richard Move. He styles his hair like hers, and he wears the same costumes and makeup. His reenactments are technically perfect, uncanny, breathtaking, and seemingly without irony. That's probably overstating it. There may be a little irony. But also not.

But I was talking about film technique. Méliès was obviously trying to be funny, and while a few directors have attempted to use miniature people to raise the dramatic stakes in a film, most have gone for comical effects. By the time you get to *Honey, I Shrunk the Kids*, you don't have much sense of any metaphysical questions, but in *The Incredible Shrinking Man,* they're very present, particularly at the end.

Surely you know the plot, but I'll reiterate it quickly. The hero, Scott Carey, is exposed to a radioactive cloud while on a boating excursion. Then he's exposed to some pesticide. The combination affects his molecular structure, and he begins to shrink. First his shirtsleeves are just a little long, but after a few days even his wife notices the difference. Then he gets his medical diagnosis, and within weeks he's the size of a five-year-old. His family is hounded by the insensitive press. Carey's doctors find an antidote that will arrest, but not reverse, his shrinkage. He meets a nice female dwarf who gives him encouragement, and he becomes determined to write his life story. But then even the treatment fails. He starts shrinking again and has to move into a dollhouse. The family cat becomes his predator, and he ends up in the basement. His wife and brother think he's lost for good. A water pipe bursts in the basement, and he struggles with a hungry spider, before skewering it with a straight pin. Finally, he's way too tiny to be found. In the last scene, the size of a speck of lint, he crawls out of the mesh of the window screen and contemplates the night sky:

> So close, the infinitesimal and the infinite; but suddenly I knew they were really the two ends of the same concept. The unbelievably small and the unbelievably vast eventually meet, like the closing of a gigantic circle. I looked up as if, somehow, I would grasp the heavens, the universe, worlds beyond number—God's silver tapestry spread across the night! And

in that moment, I knew the answer to the riddle of the infinite. I had thought in terms of man's own limited dimension. I had presumed upon nature—that existence begins and ends, is man's conception, not nature's. And I felt my body dwindling, melting, becoming nothing. My fears melted away, and in their place came—acceptance. All this vast majesty of creation, it *had* to mean something. And then I meant something too! Yes, smaller than the smallest, I meant something too. To God, there is no zero. I still exist!

S told me that the last scene was very moving to him. He made all his kids watch this film when they were little. The preview audiences had advised the producers to change the ending of the movie because it was too depressing, but they went ahead and kept it the way it was.

* * *

People have different opinions about what children should see at the movies. I may not have adequately addressed the affective force or ethical implications of *Honey, I Shrunk the Kids.* The scene where the kid is flailing around in a bowl of cereal is pretty harrowing. It also made me think a little about the catastrophic mistakes you can make as a parent. I say that as a daughter but also as a mother. Of course, it's the dad who's the bungler in *Honey, I Shrunk the Kids.* I'd have to say my own father's mistakes were probably more catastrophic than my mother's, though even he never shrank me to the size of a Cheerio. Once, though, when I was eight, he took me to his favorite dive bar, got totally hammered, and thought he could drive me home. It was very scary. He was falling down. I called my mom from the phone booth in the bar, and she told me to order him some coffee. It was 1970. People had slightly different ideas about responsible parenting in 1970. I'm sure I also made some parenting mistakes, but they're harder for me to see.

My mother was neither large nor small. She was, like me, precisely the median height for an American woman: five foot four. She was a little plump at the end of her life, and I'm a little thin, but we both were and are basically average. My mother had three miscarriages before she had me. At the time, the doctors didn't know why, but then she had to have gall bladder surgery, and they discovered some scar tissue from endometriosis that was restricting her uterus. Apparently, as her fetuses had started to grow, her uterus couldn't expand, so it pushed them out, tiny as they were. During that gall bladder operation, the doctor cut out the scar tissue as a sort of afterthought, and then my mother conceived me and was able to carry me to term. This account may not be very accurate, medically speaking, but it's the story my mother told me.

There's a beautiful song by Lhasa de Sela called "Soon This Space Will Be Too Small." I saw her perform it live once, and she said it came from something that her father had told her as a girl: that a baby remains in its mother's womb until that space is too small and it has to emerge into the world. He said that, in the same way, death was what happened when we just got too big to be in this world any longer, so we had to emerge into a different space—a bigger one. It's a very simple explanation, but I've found it comforting when thinking about death. Maybe it's true, sometimes. Lhasa de Sela died, it seems to me, far too early, of breast cancer at thirty-seven. But maybe she was just too big for this space.

That story I told about my father might make me sound a little judgmental about drinking. In fact, though I've never been much of a drinker myself and I've tended to avoid other intoxicants, I have a pretty high level of tolerance for their use by others. When I first met S—actually before I met him, when we were just beginning to correspond—he let me know about some of his habits. This was in preparation for his first visit to New York, and I realized I'd need to make some special provisions of both liquor and weed. S's relationship to alcohol is what some medical practitioners might call mildly excessive, but what he'd call French. Indeed, when we're in France, he seems to be, as I said of my mother's and my size, basically average. As for weed, well, you can chalk that up to his coming of age in May '68—and that's also probably the explanation for his other experiments with psychotropic drugs. I've certainly never seen him falling down as my father sometimes did. Well, once, but not on account of liquor. We made a road trip to Amsterdam, where, on a lark, we bought a few mysterious capsules in what appeared to be a novelty boutique for tourists. They were called Trip-E Happy Caps, and they looked like a joke. We took them just before boarding a ferry boat to a little fishing village outside of Amsterdam. We thought maybe we'd feel a little tingle, or they might slightly enhance the color of the sky. We ended up completely incapacitated. It was a nightmare. S was lying crumpled on a pier with the dry heaves. I was barely in control of my own motor functions, but I patted him on the back and somehow managed to totter back to the ferry landing to inquire about the last boat back to the mainland. S told me that as he watched me walking away from him, he saw me getting tinier and tinier, and he remembered a song by Georges Brassens that says, "*Et je l'ai vue, toute petite, partir gaiment vers mon oubli*"; "And I saw her, so tiny, happily headed off toward my forgetting." Of course, he didn't forget me, nor me him. I went back, yanked him up, draped his arm over my shoulder, and hauled him over to the ferry dock. After a series of humiliating lurches and blunders, culminating in a very expensive ride in an Uber, we made it back to our hotel room in the city, and we photographed each other's pupils, which were the size of frying pans.

I never told my son that story.

* * *

But back to the movies. Why did I say it seemed improbable that Jean Marais starred in *Amour de poche*? I always think of him in Cocteau's *La belle et la bête*—as a classical actor of highbrow cinema. *Amour de poche* is a pretty dumb romantic comedy, made in the same year as *The Incredible Shrinking Man*. It's about a scientist who wants to suspend animation. He succeeds in shrinking animals into tiny statuettes, which can be reanimated when exposed to saltwater. His cute lab assistant, who has a crush on him, shrinks herself in order to evade his jealous fiancée. Jean Marais, as the title implies, keeps her in his pocket, until the fiancée, in a fit of pique, throws her into the ocean. Marais dives into the water where he retrieves the cute assistant, full size and highly animated, and they swim away together to live, one assumes, happily ever after.

In truth, Jean Marais made a lot of popular films—many of them swashbucklers. S loves those—particularly *Le bossu*, in which he saves an eighteenth-century noblewoman (whom he's raised since infancy) by disguising himself as an old hunchback and then ripping off his costume to fence with a bunch of scoundrels. Naturally, he marries the noblewoman in the end. That film was made in 1959, and S was captivated by it as a boy. But when he speaks of why he admires Jean Marais so much, he never fails to mention Marais's deep and abiding commitment to Jean Cocteau, his lover for many years. S told me that in his autobiography, Jean Marais gave as his birth date the day he met Cocteau. S loves this kind of story—to say he's a romantic is an understatement. But this is also why it seems so strange to me that Jean Marais starred in a dumb 1957 romantic comedy about carrying a cute lab assistant around in his pocket.

To call Yve's health travails over the last year a "fantastic voyage" would be a ridiculous euphemism, but it's true that he and Sarah have been on quite a journey, having to educate themselves about the inner workings of his body. They've long been vegans, though once he was diagnosed with Crohn's they began to integrate the occasional egg or bit of fish into their diet, since he needed the protein. Their diet is largely guided by their political concerns, which include both animal rights and ecological sustainability. Sustainability—both ecological and economic—is also a theme that runs through many films featuring miniature people. As I said, radioactivity and pesticide are responsible for Scott Carey's transformation. *Downsizing* makes the connection explicit. A scientist announces: "The cause of all the catastrophes we are seeing today is overpopulation. We are proud to unveil the only practical remedy to humanity's gravest problem." It's shrinking people to 3.64 percent of their size and exiling them to Leisureland, a domed mini habitat. The allure of submitting to the procedure isn't just to save the planet; it's also to have a taste of the good life you can't quite achieve in the real world. Your piddly savings are stretched to millionaire proportions when your needs are downsized.

Pat Kramer, the protagonist of *The Incredible Shrinking Woman*, is living pretty much the "real world" version of Leisureland—apparent suburban bliss—when her unusual sensitivity to the toxicity of plastic wrap, feminine hygiene products, and artificial preservatives, among other things, initiates her shrinkage. Lily Tomlin plays a couple of side characters in that film as well, drawn from her staple TV personae, including the sanctimonious Mrs. Judith Beasley, who appears here as a saleswoman of organic products (green piety doesn't escape the satire). Tomlin also plays her famous telephone operator, but the producers cut out a scene in which she did a reprise of Edith Ann, the five-year-old character Tomlin played for years, seated on an enormous chair. Maybe they just thought it was redundant as a visual joke, since Pat Kramer also appears seated on enormous furniture.

At the end of *The Incredible Shrinking Woman*, unlike Scott Carey, Pat Kramer returns to normal size, and there's an indication that she's still growing, as her wedding band is becoming too tight. The feminist and perhaps materialist implications are pretty obvious, but I'm sorry they cut out Edith Ann for the psychoanalytic ones.

Some critics blame the lukewarm response to *The Incredible Shrinking Woman* on the screenplay, which was written by Lily Tomlin's wife, Jane Wagner. Vincent Canby's review in the *New York Times* said that Wagner was better at writing sketches than "sustained comic narrative." But, retrospectively, others have found the screenplay—as well as Wagner's other collaborative work with Tomlin—to be particularly insightful not only about feminist issues but also racial ones. Chadwick Roberts suggests that one of the film's strengths is its manner of, as Richard Dyer would put it, "making whiteness strange" (801). It also makes heterosexuality strange. You can't really unlink one from the other. Pat Kramer has a Latina domestic servant named Concepción who nearly grinds her up in the garbage disposal, unknowingly, after dousing her with the remains of the family meal. In that scene, Concepción is dancing around to salsa music, clad in spandex. Pat Kramer is dripping with raw egg and fragments of burnt toast. In *Downsizing*, racialized domestic labor is embodied in the character of Ngoc Lan Tran, played by Hong Chau, an exploited, physically maimed denizen of Leisureland. Audiences were divided on the question of whether Ngoc Lan Tran was a racial stereotype or the single nuanced character in a schlocky parody.

My mother was, as I said, an excellent housekeeper, even after she left my father and began working full time as an editor. As a single mother, I cut myself more slack in the cleaning department. But neither of us ever considered employing anybody else to take care of the kids or pick up the dirty socks. My mother's approach to what they used to call "home economics"—cooking, cleaning, sewing, and so on—was in line with her larger economic perspective. It was all about moderation and self-sufficiency. I inherited this, and this, too, I appear to have passed on to my son. When he was young, I instituted a weekly cleaning ritual, which took place on Saturdays. I vacuumed and scoured all the kitchen surfaces. He mopped the wooden floors with Murphy's Oil Soap and scrubbed down the bathroom. By Fridays, the place had usually gotten a little messy, but it always felt basically under control. I have something of an allergy to the idea of hired domestic labor. It seems to me one really ought to be able to clean up after oneself. That may make me sound like the sanctimonious Mrs. Judith Beasley. Of course, I understand why people with disabilities or particularly demanding jobs might need to do some outsourcing.

My mother, similarly, gave me and my sister "chores," but the weekly ritual in my childhood was something called "craft Sundays." Each week she'd teach us something like macramé or tatting (though not, as I mentioned, knitting), and afterward we'd have dinner at McDonald's and visit the mobile library housed in a trailer in the parking lot. We could check out two books, but we had to read them. As for the food, we could order what we wanted, but we had to finish it. This same rule held at home. We could serve ourselves, but we had to clean our plates. I still clean my plate. This is a difference between S and me. He always leaves some scraps on his. When we're in the country, he leaves these scraps outside the door for the animals.

All of the bratty kids in *Willy Wonka and the Chocolate Factory* appear to have been badly parented: too much leniency, too much TV, and of course too much sugar. The shrinking scene, as you may remember, involves an obnoxious boy named Mike Teavee who impulsively jumps onto a platform and gets zapped into a television set. He climbs out of the screen, reduced to the height of about two inches. He seems perfectly happy, but his mother is understandably disturbed. Strangely, what I hadn't remembered about the movie until I watched it again was the Oompa Loompas—Willy Wonka's short-statured minions. This appears to be a hat tip to the Munchkins of *The Wizard of Oz*. It's the Oompa Loompas who zap Mike Teavee with the teleportation device the moment he commands them to do so. They're perfectly servile. Watching it today, of course, makes you cringe. The real little people in these films are docile laborers, even more so than Concepción or Ngoc Lan Tran. Apparently, in one draft of the story, Roald Dahl made the Oompa Loompas African "Pygmies." But his wife said that Charlie, the only sympathetic kid of the bunch, was originally Black (Siddique).

When I mentioned all this to S, he told me that in the original Brothers Grimm telling of the story of Snow White and the Seven Dwarfs, the little men who come to Snow White's rescue weren't born small but became so through their exploited labor—by carrying heavy loads of ore from the mines. I looked up the original story, and I didn't find that. I did find a line I remembered, in which the dwarves tell Snow White, "If you will keep house for us, and cook, sew, make beds, wash, and knit, and keep everything clean and orderly, then you can stay here, and you'll have everything that you want" (12). But when I poked around some more, I saw that a German historian named Eckhard Sander surmised that Snow White was based on an actual sixteenth-century countess, murdered by her wicked stepmother, and that the dwarves were based on child laborers who were forced to work in her father's copper mines ("Origin of the Snow White Tale").

The other "real little people" in all these films are, of course, children.

* * *

Once, when Yve was really sick, I told him I thought of him as my "number two son." He was understandably ambivalent about that. Despite the difference in our ages, we are peers and collaborators. Also, he really loves his real mother. But I told him that my son has called me Barbara for as long as I can remember, and I also think of him as my peer and collaborator. In fact, I was just telling him that he seems to be always teaching me how to be a grown-up.

Yve's long had a conflicted relationship with his father, who's a doctor. But Yve told me that when he learned of Yve's medical situation, he cried like a baby.

As I said, I find it harder to see my own parenting mistakes. I hesitated to tell you the reason I told my son he was teaching me how to be a grown-up. I'm writing this from Normandy. S and I came here for the winter break, and a couple of days after we arrived, after I'd begun writing about miniature people in films, my son texted me to say that he needed to speak with me on the phone. There was also a text from a friend who is particularly active on social media, unlike me. That text said, ominously, "I'm so sorry to hear of Leo's dad!" I assumed the worst.

When I spoke with Leo, he told me that he'd received a call in Portland, where he's been living, saying that Tony had suffered a heart attack and died. He was swimming in a pool in Queens when it happened. He was fifty-five years old. Naturally, this was a shock, but my own emotional response was entirely focused on Leo. His father had effectively evaporated when Leo was still very small, and he moved back to Brazil. They hadn't had a lot of interaction until recent years, when

Tony seemed to want to make up for lost time. He moved to Queens. So much had happened in the interim. Tony reached out to me as well, but I didn't feel particularly compelled to reconnect. Leo was more generous. He'd spent years arranging surrogate father figures, but even he could see that it might be a good idea to try to salvage something. It was complicated, but he made an effort. Not long ago, Leo asked S if he could call him "Dad," which was funny, considering that he calls me Barbara. He called his father Tony. S was very touched by the request, but he told Leo he thought he should think of him as an older friend. It's sort of the inversion of Yve's response to my calling him my "number two son."

When Tony died, Leo again managed to muster more wisdom and maturity than I did. He flew back to New York, made the funeral arrangements, and began to attend to his father's affairs. He gently suggested that I should reach out and comfort Tony's bereaved godson, who was taking it pretty hard. That's when I told him he seemed always to be teaching me how to be a grown-up. There's a lot to say about why Tony became so tiny in my life and probably much more to say about the space he's occupied in Leo's, but that part isn't my story to tell.

Leo stayed in our apartment while he was dealing with the funeral and all the paperwork. He texted me one night and asked if I had a copy of the *Oulipo Compendium* in the apartment. I thought that was a good sign. He wanted to write. The *Oulipo Compendium* is a recipe book of writing constraints. Constraints, of course, are necessary for some of us to write. That's why Lauren Berlant and Kathleen Stewart wrote in multiples of one hundred words. Harry Mathews co-edited the *Compendium*. Harry was one of the people who'd been a sort of surrogate father for Leo. When Harry died, Leo comforted me by reciting, from memory, one of Harry's poems.

* * *

I paused here to consult with Leo. I wanted to make sure he didn't feel I'd overstepped in talking about his relationship with his father. He read a draft of this chapter, and he told me it was "a good read all around, and I quite enjoyed many of the film and literary references." Then he offered a few notes on the sections concerning him. "In truth, it was never my intention to 'salvage' any kind of relationship with Tony." He said he felt "hounded" by his father's voicemails and texts but ignoring them just exacerbated things. He mentioned a couple of times when Tony showed up unannounced at his door, "his mouth open, and his torso hunched over, muttering incoherently. That was the low point of whatever connection I tried to maintain with him. He was desperate for some form of vindication." This was probably part of the impetus for Leo's trip to Europe and for his subsequent relocation to the West Coast. Leo said the one hope he held out was that if he ever had his own child, his own "tiny me," maybe that would "snap Tony out of his obsession to revisit the past and make amends." He said that after his father died, their relationship "improved." He could breathe again and find a little understanding—"call it rosy retrospection or whatever."

I knew all that, but I didn't want to say it. I also didn't want to say that Tony had received the same psychiatric diagnosis as my own father. I told Leo, "It's funny, I seem to have no compunction about talking about my own father's weakness, but I didn't want to talk about Tony's. Like I said, I thought maybe that was your story to tell."

He said, "Maybe you could quote me," so I did. He told me I was right about the *Oulipo Compendium*. He wrote some other things. I think he'll write more.

* * *

It seems to me that the saddest thing about the end of *The Incredible Shrinking Man* isn't Carey's disappearing—it's that he's gotten too small to wield a pencil. That's surely evidence of my own disproportionate sense of things. Still, writing down his life story is the one thing that gives Carey hope during that period when he's child size. Throughout much of the film, his voice-overs are implicitly taken from the autobiography he's been drafting. At the end, of course, that's impossible. But maybe giving up on being a writer is part of the great dilation that his contraction made possible. I have a feeling that's one of the reasons S finds it so moving. He's often told me that his own father's frustrated ambitions of being a writer of note led him to reject those same ambitions in his own regard, although he's compulsively kept a journal all his life, and many people—myself included—have tried to encourage him to publish his contemplative writings. His father was also a remarkable thinker and writer. S showed me a letter from Jean Cocteau saying as much. But the world of publishing doesn't have, and never had, cosmic proportions. Who wrote that text at the end of the film? It wasn't Scott Carey. It was a novelist named Richard Matheson. He was working with his son, also named Richard, on an updated version of *The Incredible Shrinking Man* when he died in 2013. I wonder if it made his son feel small to be the son of the man who wrote *The Incredible Shrinking Man*.

.

suite for toy piano

....

My son began taking piano lessons when he was seven years old. At the time, I was a visiting professor at Tulane University, and New Orleans seemed like a good place for Leo to begin his musical education. Through friends, I found a teacher—a low-key bluesman whom I suspected might be a good match. He told me that not everybody was born to play piano, so he'd let me know after the first lesson if it made sense for Leo to continue. Happily, it did. Leo took to the instrument like a fish to water. Actually, it was only at his lessons that he got to play a real piano. At home, he practiced on an electronic keyboard. I got one with eighty-eight weighted keys, so at least it felt sort of like the real thing. Even though he was only seven, the recommendation was that he get used to the size and feel of a full-sized instrument as soon as possible. His teacher told me right away that he seemed to have a "nice touch." That's probably the phrase I've most often heard people use regarding his playing over the years.

It was only years later, when he was in a performing arts high school, long after we'd invested in a pretty good used Yamaha upright, that I decided to give him a toy piano. Obviously, this wasn't an educational toy. It was sort of a joke, but also not. By that time, he was already over six feet tall. He'd totter with his skinny ass on the tiny bench, knees bent up around his ears, and clink away, with minor frustration but some delight, at the twenty-five keys. It was a Schoenhut "traditional" spinet. I made one weird video of him noodling on it in the tub (no water, only naked from the waste up, playing "The Girl from Ipanema"). He also indulged me in a collaboration on a cover of Léo Ferré's "La vie d'artiste" in which he banged out a tinkled version of Ferré's crazed massacre of the keys while I croaked the closing diatribe:

> Je continue ma vie d'artiste!
> Plus tard, sans trop savoir pourquoi,
> Un étranger, un maladroit,
> Lisant mon nom sur une affiche,
> Te parlera de mes succès,
> Mais un peu triste toi, qui sais:
> "Tu lui diras que je m'en fiche…
> Que je m'en fiche…"

> I'll carry on with my life as an artist!
> Later, without really knowing why,
> A stranger, an awkward blunderer,
> Reading my name on a poster,
> Will talk to you about my successes,
> But a bit sad, you, who know [will say]:

"You'll tell him that I don't give a damn…
That I don't give a damn…."

It was ironic, of course, but not really. Maybe for both of us.

Eventually, Leo lent the toy piano to his best friend, who was, like him, a John Cage enthusiast. The friend started performing with it, and Leo never bothered to ask him to give it back.

* * *

I hadn't thought much about the Schoenhut for a while, until a little over a year ago, when I received an email inviting me to speak at the Dutch Art Institute. The invitation came from an instructor at the institute with whom I'd previously corresponded on the topic of fictocriticism, a generic moniker that's been applied to the kind of writing that this person and I sometimes do. My colleague told me that he'd assigned one of my novels in the course he was teaching and that it had provoked some lively debates among his students. There were three of them, in particular, who'd expressed an interest in asking me some questions about what it means to construct a fictional, or semifictional, narrative out of one's research on artistic practice. He wondered if I might visit the DAI, give a presentation on my work, and then engage in a public conversation with his students.

I had already gleaned that the educational strategies of the DAI were rather unusual. On its website, it's described as a "soft spaceship," which, a few years ago, divested itself of bricks and mortar, instituting a "roaming academy" for students working at the intersection of performance art and critical theory. Their classes, that is, are held at "various locations in and around Europe, with recurring moorings at selected stations in the East and (rural) South Netherlands." Regarding the research concerns of the participants, the "DAI positions itself as a left-leaning program with a feminist, intersectional, anti-capitalist and decolonial orientation." (The website acknowledges that this is perhaps easier said than done, given the institute's imbrication in European history.)

Well, if these young artists were curious about me, the feeling was, of course, mutual. I decided to accept the invitation, but first to perform a little research on my proposed interlocutors. The only clues I'd been given were their names and their pronouns of preference: Julian Fricker, Risa Horn, and … Zachary Schoenhut. They, she, they.

I began poking around. The first of the three was, quite literally, shrouded in mystery. Unless, of course, the Julian Fricker in question was a sixth-tier footballer playing for FSV Jägersburg. That's what I came up with in my initial Google search. It seemed possible but somehow improbable. This Fricker's age seemed about right, and they might technically have been termed a "performance artist," as several websites supplied "detailed performance data," indicating, for example, eleven appearances, two yellow cards, and a single goal. But none of this struck me as the kind of performance that would have led the young artist to a soft spaceship of experimentalism.

After that first false start, all I could find was a Craft CMS Beta page (since deleted) that told me, "Apparently, this user prefers to keep an air of mystery about them." The "user," that is, had provided nary a hint of their personal identity. Their avatar, from a distance, resembled a white bat, but when I zoomed in, I realized it was actually a more disconcerting image than that: a gust of vapor and debris following an apparently massive detonation among skyscrapers. I wasn't sure if the image was shot from above or below, which of course added to my disorientation. According to this ephemeral trace on the internet, Julian Fricker had supplied "0" answers and only "1" question. But what WAS the question?

Stumped, I turned to Risa Horn. Here, suddenly, the path became much clearer—or at least seemed to. Evidence abounded. Google Books led me to the indelible imprint of Frau Risa Horn, amply documented in the literature on Viennese modernist art, 1890–1914. As the art historian Tag Gronberg noted, Risa Horn was forever immortalized by Peter Altenberg in photographs and text published in the "lavish, upmarket" journal *Kunst.* Altenberg waxed particularly lyrical on "the hand of sweet Mrs. Risa Horn": "Hand, hand, noblest, most delicate object, you, artwork of God, when can one see you?" (*"Wann erblickt man dich?"*) "For years and years, one's seen paws and claws, clumsy, bulky shapes, as if formed by childish artists disrespectful of the flesh!... O beautiful, light, tender, gentle hands, noblest works of nature, where are you? Beautiful, noble, delicate hands should be erected as altars, for they are creations, stemming from the spirit of God! Mrs. Risa H., for the grace of God, save your noble hands!" (cited in Gronberg, 110). (That's my own clumsy, bulky translation.)

Well, there may be some rhetorical excess in all that, but this much is true: in the photos, Frau Risa Horn's hand looked pretty good.

Finally, there was Zachary Schoenhut. Zachary's trail was fleeting but enchanting! I almost felt I ought to hold

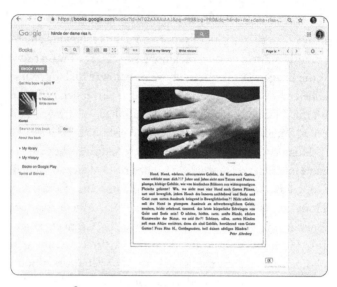

fig 4.1 Hand, Hand…(Google Books)

my breath to get a glimpse of them. There were a few videos online—one depicting (apparently) Zachary, shot from afar, scampering at the margins of a pale green field dressed in a flouncy pink nightgown. They'd flit into view momentarily and then scuttle out again. I could hear intermittent smidgens of their elfin laughter in the distance.

But if Zachary's trajectory was ethereal, I thought, *perhaps*, their origins were in fact of an illustrious, legendary, even fabled stature. Could they be the scion of the Schoenhut toy piano dynasty? It seemed to me a possibility almost too tantalizing to consider. "Zachary," I wondered, "did you also grow up surrounded by tiny things? Did they make you feel small—or on the contrary, did they make you feel, by contrast, enormous?"

I imagined Zachary very little, comfortable, maybe, in a world where the objects were apportioned, just right, for their little fingers and limbs. But then, like Alice after she ate the cake, they must have started growing, and maybe they felt constrained. Maybe even the tinkling keys, in all their bell-like purity and innocence, began to irk them. Maybe that sound made them anxious. Maybe that's why they felt compelled to fly away, far away, to that soft spaceship. . . .

But maybe not. Maybe Zachary still loved delicacy, and the sound of bell-like tinkling. There was a hint that might be true. Another video, a dainty one, the camera's eye focused, lovingly, on a ruby earring, nestled like a ladybug on the lobe of a pretty young girl, shot in profile, as she chewed on something. There was nothing unflattering about her eating. She was shot in slow motion, discreetly, lovingly, with a fragile accompaniment on what sounded like chimes.

Does all this make me sound like an internet stalker? An incompetent, misguided sleuth? Or just another soft-boiled performatic cosmonaut, stumbling on oddball connections that I might metabolize into a work of fiction that indicated—what?—a hunger to make some sort of connection, even with people who might not really exist or might not be who they seemed to be? Is that what we call a fictocritic?

None of this is really new. My colleague at the DAI had suggested I might historically frame a narrative approach to performance analysis for his students. All kinds of genealogies are possible, but I thought it might be more telling for me to offer

fig 4.2
"Queering"
(Z. Schoenhut)

a very personal one; I think I must have been about nineteen when I first read *Nadja* by André Breton. It changed everything for me. Today, when I teach that book to my students, they're often put off by what they perceive as Breton's masculine bombast, or worse, by the cruel disregard for the fate of a woman that they read in the story—both that recounted in the novel and that which they find in researching the life of the "real" Nadja, Léona Camile Ghislaine Delacourt. Maybe you know that story, or those stories. Breton encounters a young woman by chance on a street in Paris. She tells him her name is Nadja but also says that that name is made-up and that she took it from the Russian word for hope: "надежда" (66).

Despite the optimism inscribed in that gesture of self-fictionalization, things don't go very well for Nadja. There's a series of meetings between her and Breton in which they exchange work, anecdotes, and other intimacies, some physical, one nearly fatal. "One evening," Breton writes, "when I was driving a car along the road from Versailles to Paris, the woman sitting beside me (who was Nadja, but who might have been anyone else, after all, *someone else*) pressed her foot down on mine on the accelerator, tried to cover my eyes with her hands in the oblivion of an interminable kiss, desiring to extinguish us, doubtless forever, save to each other, so that we should collide at full speed with the splendid trees along the road" (152). By the end of the book, she's been institutionalized, diagnosed as psychotic. Breton does some handwringing over the pathologizing of people, like Nadja, who might be said to live in a liminal space between fiction and reality, but she remained institutionalized for fourteen years, until her death at the age of thirty-nine. I understand why some of my students read her as the sacrificial lamb in Breton's telling of things and why the highly gendered position of ill-fated "muse" makes them balk. But the story of the car trip from Versailles to Paris might make anyone feel ill-equipped to take full responsibility for Nadja's care.

I told you how scary it was to get in the car with my father.

* * *

My father also loved the piano. His name was also Leo. He had an old upright in his apartment, which was otherwise furnished with some rickety lawn chairs and a folding card table strewn with dirty cups and plastic spoons. The place reeked of cigarettes and instant coffee. During one spring break in college, I decided to make a pilgrimage to visit him. When I arrived, he nonchalantly opened the door and introduced me to his other visitor, seated on one of the lawn chairs. He was a tiny man with a combover, and my father told me his name was Mr. Moto. I guess this was a joke, but Mr. Moto and I just nodded at each other, and shortly after that he discreetly took his leave. There was no further explanation. I think they were probably friends from AA.

My father wasn't much of a musician, but he was an expert listener, and his use of the piano was mostly just to figure out what chords other people were playing on the records he listened to throughout the day. Though he'd been trained as an urban sociologist, and had once had some standing in the field, after he'd been basically incapacitated by his psychiatric and substance-related difficulties, his occasional writings were limited to erotic poems and appreciations of the jazz pianists he loved the most. He managed to publish one essay in 1968 (during a manic phase, just before the shit hit the fan)—on Oscar Peterson as the carrier of Art Tatum's legacy—but for years the musician he listened to most reverently was Bill Evans. I think my father's love of Bill Evans was a combination of empathy regarding Evans's addiction and a genuine admiration of his playing.

Bill Evans also had a nice touch.

* * *

When the time came for my guest lecture, I got on an airplane to Amsterdam and, on landing, followed the detailed instructions of my DAI administrative liaison, boarding a swift and pristine Thalys train to Antwerp. I was told to go to the Starbucks in the train station to meet a curator and conceptual artist named Margret. I was furnished in advance with her photograph—a blonde woman of about my age with architectural eyeglasses. We would both be picked up in a van by someone named Jacqu. Margret and I chitchatted for a while on the Starbucks banquette. We were not questioned about our occupation of the banquette, although we hadn't ordered anything and were there for a while. A pair of policemen did, however, poke at a migrant who had stretched out on another banquette in order to sleep. He assumed a seated position, which seemed to satisfy them.

When Jacqu arrived, she turned out to be a woman, slightly frazzled and apologetic (she was about an hour late—traffic). She and Margret, who was a regular instructor at the institute, sat up front, and I sat in the back and nodded off briefly. We arrived after dark in Nieuwvliet, a small fishing village where the spaceship had temporarily moored. I was shown to the cottage that Margret and I would be sharing (modern and sparsely furnished, with separate bedrooms) to drop my bag, and then to a communal dinner in another house (mussels and excellent wine). It turned out that I knew a few of the other faculty members—not just that colleague who'd invited me, but also a very dear Greek former student of mine and another friend of a friend, an American anarchist writer whose work I knew well. I was exhausted, so after filling up on mussels and a big glass of that excellent wine, I toddled off, leaving Margret to kibitz with the others.

The next morning, we were summoned to a bus, which would take us all—faculty and students—to an abandoned medieval church, where there would be some crits of the students' work. Although my own talk wouldn't take place until the next day, I was invited to be a respondent at these crits. There was a sound installation, accompanied by aromas, which worked very beautifully with the acoustics of the old church and its intrinsic scents of stone and old wood. There was an elaborate interactive performance that involved carefully handcrafted game pieces and live image projections. Much of the art these students had made struck one as being meticulously conceived and constructed, and perhaps intentionally hermetic. Some of it was quite explicit in its intentions. I hazarded some interpretive associations on the opaquer ones and asked questions about the more obvious ones.

Naturally, I was looking around, trying to guess which of the students in the audience were the ones I'd be conversing with. None of them were showing work in these crits. During the lunch break (vegan stew, ladled into bowls and eaten at long tables), someone introduced me to Julian, who needless to say was *not* the FSV footballer. A very warm and self-possessed young woman came and put her hand on my shoulder, saying she was looking forward to our discussion. I surmised that this was Risa and said I was also excited. Zachary was the only one I'd managed to glimpse on video, so I was pretty sure I'd spotted them in the crowd. As if intuiting this, they merely smiled at me from a distance, nodding discreetly. Then, as the rest of us slogged away at our vegan stew, Zachary Schoenhut mounted a little stage that held a (full-sized) upright piano and began playing Debussy. When I saw them sit down at the piano and begin to pick out—not with any particular expertise, in fact—the notes of "Clair de lune," tears spontaneously spouted out of my eyes. I badly missed my son.

The day of crits was long, so the organizers had gently scheduled a break for me in the middle of the day, after that lunch. An Italian art critic was taking over as the respondent for a while. It was cool but sunny, so I strolled around the area. People in the Netherlands appear to think of the street-facing windows of their homes as display cases. It was difficult to distinguish private residences from antique stores or flower shops. This is most common, of course, on the ground floor, but some homes even carried out the practice on the higher stories. I found myself gazing up for some time at a second-floor window peopled with porcelain-headed dolls. They gazed right back at me.

The next day, we boarded a bus to Antwerp, where we would be mooring at a converted former shipbuilding hangar on the piers, but our departure was delayed by a very disturbing encounter. Nieuwvliet, the little fishing village where we'd

fig 4.3 Dutch Window (B. Browning)

briefly docked, apparently didn't get the memo about Zwarte Piet, a folkloric character who is ostensibly one of Santa's—or Sinterklaas's—little helpers. The character was popularized in a nineteenth-century children's book by a schoolteacher named Jan Schenkman. As reported in the pages of *Al Jazeera*, "Black Pete" was now considered by many to be "Dutch racism on full display." As the Christmas season approached, locals would put on blackface, don renaissance costumes, and tool around, passing out candy to local children. In truth, I hadn't gotten the memo either—I'd never heard of Zwarte

Piet, so I was really thrown for a loop when a golf cart pulled up alongside the bus we'd boarded and its blackface occupants started trying to hand out candy. These were not, needless to say, performance artists with a feminist, intersectional, anti-capitalist, and decolonial orientation.

The students and faculty members of the DAI are an international lot, and several scrambled out of our bus to confront the locals, but it was only the Dutch-speaking ones who could really engage these people in a dialogue about what was wrong with their antics. In fact, I think there was only one Dutch student in the group, and she was clearly rattled by the incident. We watched as she threw her hands in the air and shouted, in tears, at the befuddled candy-distributers, who didn't have a clue. When I later read about Zwarte Piet in *Al Jazeera,* I learned that there had been massive protests just days before in Eindhoven and Rotterdam, among other urban areas, with some very aggressive and racist right-wing counter-protests. The Nieuwvliet crew didn't put up much resistance, just saying they'd been doing this for years and it never seemed to have hurt anybody's feelings. They sort of apologized, and drove their golf cart back to wherever they'd come from, but the whole encounter had left the busload of us in a funk. The Dutch woman was seated behind me, next to a Black British guy. She was traumatized, and he seemed to be trying to comfort her by explaining that this kind of thing happens all over the world, and he didn't waste too much time or emotional energy trying to engage ignorant people in a conversation about the racism they refused to see in themselves. The rest of the trip was mostly passed in silence.

* * *

That trip to visit my father in the 1980s was something of a catastrophe—or maybe it wasn't. I don't know what I was expecting, really. I'd scrimped and saved up the cost of the airplane ticket from my dining-hall job as a dishwasher and had just enough to scrape by for the week I'd be crashing there. Shortly after Mr. Moto left, my father passed me, with a wan smile, what appeared to be a crisp, carefully folded fifty-dollar bill. I was touched and a little surprised, as he also wasn't rolling in dough. Later, when I ventured out to buy a few provisions, I unfolded it and realized it was a joke: a toy bill, only two-thirds the length of actual legal tender. I don't know where he got the toy money—maybe from Mr. Moto. For most of my visit, my father was fairly catatonic. I also wasn't so good at making small talk. We listened to a lot of Bill Evans. I had to go out periodically and walk around on account of the cigarette smoke.

* * *

Once the DAI crew arrived at the hangar on the piers, the mood started to lift. We wandered around the hangar for a while, and then I was told to go up to a staged area with a domestic tableau: a sofa, a rug, a coffee table, and a movie screen. This was where I was to deliver my lecture. In it, I presented Julian, Risa, and Zachary (and everyone else) with the half-baked stories I'd concocted out of their "real" and associative traces on the internet. That, along with a few references to Breton and Zora Neale Hurston, constituted the bulk of my talk, which was accompanied by a slideshow I'd constructed out of the images and footage I'd collected online. There was also an image of Alice in Wonderland, enormous, disgruntled, with her massive arm sticking out the window of an overly confining house after having eaten her calamitous cake. When I finished talking, the three students joined me on the sofa for our discussion.

It seemed I wasn't so far askew of reality as I'd thought.

Julian, it turned out, was precisely the kind of person to whom I'd be tempted to write, as Breton once wrote to his own daughter, "I want you to be madly loved"—though really, one wouldn't need to say it. I'm pretty sure they already are, have been, and will be loved to the point of rapture. Julian does drag performances under the moniker Shiaz Legz. Indeed, they have legs, and they're exquisite, but so is everything else about them. If I tell you Julian is a drag performer, you may think that their splendor relies on makeup and glitter. There was plenty of that in their performance art, which I later got a chance to see, but even barefaced, Julian was heartbreakingly beautiful—and more than that, clearly gentle, empathetic, and wise. I'd had evidence of that the day before. During the session of crits, when I stepped out for that brief walk around the grounds of the medieval church, there'd been an incident. When I returned from my stroll, one of the students was in tears, having been, it seems, skewered by the other visiting dignitary, that Italian art critic. The student's peers sprang to her defense, but the mood was dark, and Julian discreetly pulled me aside to explain, in a hushed voice, and with subtle insight, what had happened. Actually, that incident also had something to do with race. The student had presented a piece about racist questions that had been directed at her regarding her food art (why did she not produce Asian cuisine?), and the Italian critic had found her interpretation of those questions to be overly sensitive. Sensitivity, of course, is relative and depends on certain factors.

But back to my interlocutors. Risa, of course, was not the muse of the Viennese modernists. She was, as I said, a gracious, composed young woman—American, thoroughly contemporary, with a penetrating gaze and a razor-sharp intellect. But astonishingly, after I'd finished my bizarre account of her ostensible inspiration of Altenberg, she told me that, in fact, she *had* worked as a hand model. That made my mouth drop open. Her questions, though, had nothing to do with any of that. She wanted to talk about Marcel Mauss, and the nature of gift economies, and the ways artists might intervene in the political economy. These happen to be passionate interests of mine as well, and we probably could have chewed the Maussian fat for hours. Unfortunately, our conversation was cut short by the conveners of the symposium.

While both Julian and Risa had turned out to be elegant, compelling people, you will have understood that my greatest curiosity had been piqued by the prospect of meeting Zachary Schoenhut. That was only partly due to the fact that I was reasonably sure I'd actually unearthed some of Zachary's own work. That work was intriguing, all right, but it was the plausibility of the toy piano dynasty hypothesis that really got me going. In Googling Zachary, I'd found a page dedicated to the Schoenhut Family Foundation, a grantmaking organization whose president and vice president appeared to be Zachary's parents. Zachary and what I presumed to be their siblings were listed as directors, each working for an hour per week, with no compensation. There was, it seemed, *some* sort of family dynasty.

Could it be this one? Albert Schoenhut was born in Württemberg, Germany, in 1848. Both his grandfather and his father were toymakers, specializing in wooden dolls, rocking horses, and the like. Albert joined the family business, but he quickly developed a particular interest in toy pianos. At the time, the *Kinderklavier* was generally made with glass sounding bars struck by hammers, but Albert began using more durable, metal bars. Toy pianos were very popular with German families, and those who emigrated to the United States often brought them along. But the instruments didn't always survive the transatlantic crossing—particularly if they had glass sounding bars. Wanamaker's Department Store in Philadelphia (today, Macy's) heard about Albert's technical stills, and they arranged for him to come to the United States to work as a repairman, replacing broken pieces. He was seventeen years old when he arrived. Albert worked for Wanamaker's for six years and then left to found A. Schoenhut and Company, which also manufactured xylophones and glockenspiels, as well as nonmusical toys. But the company's signature item was the toy piano.

A. Schoenhut and Company started out in a storefront on Frankford Avenue and then moved to a larger facility at 621–23 Adams Street (now Hagert Street). By the time the twentieth century rolled around, Albert had 125 employees, with warehouses and an office down the block from the factory. Albert had six sons, and five of them joined the company: Albert F., William G., Harry E., Gustav A., and Otto F. (I don't know if he had any daughters, and I found no information regarding Mrs. Schoenhut.) The factory grew to five stories and four hundred employees by 1907. Albert died in 1912, and the company was acquired by a series of owners, but things plugged along nicely enough until the Great Depression hit. The company declared bankruptcy in 1935. That's when Otto F. scrounged up a business partner, Stanley Osborn, and they started a new company, O. Schoenhut Inc. Their big seller in the new economy was a significantly more modest toy: 456 Pick Up Sticks (those remained a hit for twenty years).

Otto didn't invent pick-up sticks—he just made a particularly popular version of them. In fact, if you research the origins of pick-up sticks, you find some contradictory information. Some people say it was a First Nations game. Some people say it came from China. There are other names for the toy: among them, jackstraws, spillikins, and Mikado. Ironically, "Mikado" is the version that Wikipedia claims originated in Europe. "In 1936, it was brought from Hungary (where it was called Marokko) to the United States and named pick-up sticks.... The game is named for the highest scoring (blue) stick 'Mikado' (Emperor of Japan)." That seems to have something to do with nineteenth-century *Japonisme.*

Pick Up Sticks kept Otto's company afloat for a while. Eventually, people started buying toy pianos again.

* * *

In 1912, the year of Albert Schoenhut's death, his sons published a catalog commemorating not his demise but rather the fortieth anniversary of his arrival in the United States and his career repairing and then manufacturing toys here. They attributed the success of his signature product to its being "true to life"—a realistic, if miniature, version of an adult piano. "Before that time," they wrote, "toys were fanciful creations, obeying no law other than the mind of the toy maker. But deep down in the heart of every child is the passion for *real* life, for *true* stories." That was fascinating. It also made me think of Frances Glessner Lee.

I read that quote in an article by Patricia Simpson, a professor of German literature and an authority on the history of the German immigrant community. Her reading of Albert Schoenhut and his family focused on Albert's "preoccupation with realism, which could be interpreted as culturally German, [yet] was seen by some, not least his own sons, as contributing to the Americanization of play" (Simpson). By Americanization, they apparently meant the representation of certain cultural specificities. It was Schoenhut who first produced toy soldiers with blue costumes, corresponding to the uniforms of the US military prior to 1902 (most famously during the Civil War). But Simpson also notes that while Schoenhut's toys, like all toys, tended to regulate not only national behaviors but also gender play, the company maximized its market by suggesting that girls, too, might be interested, for example, in toy airplanes. The toy pianos were not marketed toward any particular gender, but it seems they—not the soldiers nor the airplanes—represented the epitome of "realism." On that term, Simpson has a footnote: "Realism, both as a literary and artistic mode of representation, dominated the nineteenth-century aesthetic. The novels of Charles Dickens, Leo Tolstoy, and Theodor Fontane segued into the technical advances in photography and film. Theorists from Georg Lukács, Walter Benjamin, and, more recently, Fredric Jameson and Jean

Baudrillard have alerted us to the truth and fiction of realism as an articulation of objectivity." That double-bind of "truth and fiction" runs somehow parallel to the double-bind of the Schoenhuts' Germanic and American identity. I also thought about what all that had to do with "fictocriticism."

* * *

In 2007, Torben Jenk of the Frankford Historical Society posted an update on an internet site devoted to the history of manufacturing in Philadelphia. He noted that the old Schoenhut factory on Adams/Hagert Street was demolished in 1996 and was "now mostly a vacant lot north to Letterly Street. A sliver of the party wall remains attached to the house to the west (#2213). Neighbors remember the building being used to make furniture frames, but not upholstery" (Workshop of the World). Nobody seems to remember anything about toy pianos.

* * *

After I gave my half-baked lecture on that staged sofa in the former shipbuilding hangar in Antwerp, before another of those communal meals, I worked up the courage to ask Zachary a few questions, in private. They maintained the same discreet and enigmatic smile they'd flashed at me from across the medieval church. I'd had the sense that their piano playing that day had been a subtle, coded message to me. So, when I had the chance, I asked them. How close was I? Zachary said, "I don't think there's anything I can tell you about me that you that you didn't already figure out. That picture of Alice really said it all." I said, "Then you really are part of the toy piano dynasty?" Zachary's smile was a little melancholy. "In truth, no, but when I was a child, I always wanted to believe I was. I had a Schoenhut baby grand."

Different Schoenhut dynasty, perhaps without the penchant for realism. Unless, of course, you take into account "the truth and fiction of realism as an articulation of objectivity" theorized by Lukács, Benjamin, Jameson, and Baudrillard.

* * *

I began writing this chapter in early 2020, just a month or so after my son's father died. Then suddenly the pandemic hit, and I stopped writing. As I mentioned, my son had been living for the past few months in Portland, working in a piano store. He was the "media" guy, meaning the owner had hired him to take photos and to make videos of himself playing all the beautiful grand pianos they had for sale. He posted the videos on YouTube and on Facebook. When things started to get weird and scary, I stopped working on this book. I was mostly sanitizing, freaking out about S's risk factors (sixty-eight, emphysema), figuring out how to teach a class on Zoom, and strategizing cockamamie, utopian mutual-aid projects with colleagues and students. Actually, some of those turned out to be fairly functional. Of course, I called my son from time to time, but he was a little blue and sometimes didn't want to talk. When I missed him, I'd watch his videos. The piano store closed for a while, but he hadn't been working there long enough to collect unemployment. The owner of the piano store liked him, and as soon as he could, he let Leo start going back in to make more videos, alone, in the empty store.

I wondered how Zachary and Julian and Risa were holding up. I didn't know if they'd remained in Europe and, if so, how the soft spaceship of the DAI was navigating the shifting tide of border crossings. I also wondered if the global response to George Floyd's death had changed any of the discussions around race in the Netherlands. It seems it might have. The prime minister, Mark Rutte, had defended the Zwarte Piet traditions the year before and published a controversial letter, "Doe normaal of ga weg" ("Act normal or go away"), saying that anyone who called "ordinary Dutch people" racist should leave the country (Nielsen). But when protests began in the Netherlands this summer, Rutte stated publicly that racism was also a "systemic problem" there, and he was reported to have changed his mind about Zwarte Piet (Darroch). I'm not sure if that Italian art critic was having a moment of soul-searching. Of course, "soul-searching" may not be a precise description of what happened to Mark Rutte. Perhaps that metaphor of navigating shifting tides would be more accurate.

Julian and I had exchanged a couple of warm emails after our encounter, but when I tried reaching out to them a few weeks ago, they didn't answer. I asked that colleague of mine for Zachary's email, and my colleague said he believed that Zachary must be graduating from the DAI just about now. When I wrote Zachary, I congratulated them on that and mentioned that I had started and then stopped writing this story but I hoped to get back to it now. I said, "If you're inclined, send word, even briefly!" but I didn't hear back.

Nobody seemed to have Risa's email address. If you click on the contact tab on her website, it just directs you to the online *Merriam-Webster* and the definition of *contact*, which reads, in part:

1 a: union or junction of surfaces

//Cooling begins when the lava makes *contact* with the air.

b: the apparent touching or mutual tangency of the limbs of
two celestial bodies or of the disk of one body with the
shadow of another during an eclipse, transit, or occultation

c (1): the junction of two electrical conductors through
which a current passes

(2): a special part made for such a junction

//The camera's flash wasn't working because the electrical
contacts needed to be cleaned.

2 a: ASSOCIATION, RELATIONSHIP

//students and teachers in daily *contact*

b: CONNECTION, COMMUNICATION

//I lost *contact* with her years ago.

c: an establishing of communication with someone or an ob-
serving or receiving of a significant signal from a person
or object

//radar *contact* with Mars

3: a person serving as a go-between, messenger, connection,
or source of special information

//business *contacts*

4 : CONTACT LENS

//She wears *contacts* more often than glasses.

I don't know if Risa wears contacts. I can't ask her. I lost
contact with her months ago. I lost contact with all of them
months ago.

gulliver phantasies

....

I first encountered the work of Phyllis Greenacre while preparing a lecture on D. W. Winnicott for a course I was teaching on theories of the fetish object. Winnicott held that the "transitional object," as he theorized it—which could be anything from the infant's own thumb to a blanket or toy that a child found indispensable—was not the same as a sexual fetish (5), but Greenacre pushed the connection a little further, arguing that perhaps a fetish object was a transitional object "gone awry" (144). In Winnicott's theory, manipulation of the transitional object is the child's way of coming to terms with individuation—it's the child's "not-me," but also their "not not-me." It's what allows one to get used to the idea of separation from things—particularly from one's mother.

I love Winnicott, but I've always been a little disappointed by his dodging of the question of the sexual or erotic aspects of all this. He describes the thumb-sucking infant as being in "quiet union" with him or herself (1)—which I find very moving. The "union" seems to me to respond to the various cutting figures that are used, from Aristophanes in Plato's *Symposium* to Sigmund Freud in his consideration of the castration complex, to describe one's sense of having been or possibly being severed from some part of oneself. The early transitional objects, those that come after the thumb, Winnicott notes, aren't marked by gender, though later, "boys to some extent tend to go over to use hard objects, whereas girls tend to proceed right ahead to the acquisition of a family" (4). That's an interesting way of describing what's clearly playing with dolls. "The acquisition of a family." He doesn't really talk about the process of socialization in that transition. There's also not much on what those "hard objects" are, though one might surmise they include toy cars and guns, as well as the Schoenhut airplanes, even though they were marketed to girls.

As for Winnicott's disinclination to address sexual play, he claims that in "real" play, sexual excitation is held at bay because there should be no climax. Any little girl who remembers rocking on a rocking horse knows that while there may not have been any climax, it could certainly involve sexual excitation. When I emphasize, or perhaps overemphasize, this aspect of play in my teaching, I sometimes inadvertently apologize for overdoing it by saying that it's my "hobby horse."

In 1969, Phyllis Greenacre wrote an essay in "homage" to Winnicott, extending his insights. It was titled "The Fetish and the Transitional Object," and in it, Greenacre noted:

> The transitional object and the fetish resemble each other in certain formal aspects: both are inanimate objects adopted and utilized by the individual to aid in maintaining a psychophysical balance under conditions of more or less strain. But there are rather striking differences in their origins and roles.

The transitional object appears in and belongs to infancy, and is generally relinquished when infancy merges into childhood. The fetish, on the other hand, is commonly adopted as a necessary prop or adjunct to insure adequate sexual performance in adult life.... [But] there are other fetishistic phenomena in which the differences from the transitional object are not so clear-cut. (144)

For one thing, according to Greenacre, the fetish, like the transitional object, can contain "congealed anger" (162). I like that phrase. Winnicott acknowledged that children often mutilate their beloved toys. That's part of their investment in them. In 2005, Dr. Agnes Nairn did a study in Bath, England, of girls who mutilated their Barbie dolls—a surprisingly common phenomenon. Dr. Nairn noted that among these girls, "The types of mutilation are varied and creative, and range from removing the hair to decapitation, burning, breaking and even microwaving." Nairn claimed that the mutilation was the girls' way of combating rampant consumerism. Anastasia de Waal, a journalist at the *Guardian,* thought Nairn was overstating her case. Despite the fact that they're marketed to girls, Barbies are hard. But Winnicott gives examples of brutal acts of aggression against blankets and teddy bears.

Anyway, all of this is a digression. What I really wanted to tell you about was another work by Phyllis Greenacre—*Swift and Carroll: A Psychoanalytic Study of Two Lives.* It was her first monograph, a psychoanalytic study of two authors who presented the best-known literary depictions of miniature (as well as gigantic) people. I read it around the time I started writing my little fictocritical piece about Zachary Schoenhut, after I was reminded of *Alice's Adventures in Wonderland*. I poked around and found out that Greenacre had written this book, though it was out of print. I ordered an old copy online, and while I was waiting for it to arrive, I read an essay by Sándor Ferenczi, written in 1926, titled "Gulliver Phantasies." S had turned me on to Ferenczi a few years ago. As I said, S was deeply moved by *Thalassa*, where Ferenczi argued that one's desire to return to the amniotic comfort of the womb was a residual impulse, shared by all species, to return to the sea, from which all life sprang. Sex, he said, was nothing other than that.

S is currently deep into the naturalist Rachel Carson's *The Sea around Us*. Carson is better known for *Silent Spring,* her 1962 book which spurred the environmental movement in this country. Two years after *Silent Spring* was published, Carson died of breast cancer. S has always had an interest in naturalist writings, but his hunger for them has increased in recent months, since we've been confined to a New York City apartment. He'd intended to go back to Normandy in April—partly to take care of the little house there, partly to get a break from New York, but mostly to see his two daughters. He'd planned to bring the younger one back with him on her eighteenth birthday. Of course, those flights were all canceled. Then we started hoping that by midsummer we'd be able to go together, and then those hopes were dashed. Now it's entirely unclear when either of us could go. When he writes to the French consulate, they're singularly unhelpful. It seems some French citizens can travel there if they demonstrate an emergency, but I'm not French, and even if S could convince them of his own emergency status, he's worried he wouldn't be able to come back here, and a prolonged separation isn't really thinkable for either of us. Plus, of course, a sixty-eight-year-old with emphysema is really not advised to take a long airplane trip right now or for the foreseeable future.

We sit on the balcony and try to pretend it's the deck of a ship. We try to see the city lights like stars, but of course they're not stars. We're growing some plants out there, and a small family of pigeons made a nest in one planter, so I guess that sort of counts as wildlife. S really misses the country but not nearly as much as he misses his daughters.

I loved *Thalassa*, and I ended up passing it along to a student of mine named Annie. I also gave Annie *The Animal Family* by Randall Jarrell—a favorite of mine in childhood. The parents in that family are a hunter and a mermaid, who don't really have sex as we generally construe it (she, of course, has a fish tail). They adopt their children, who are all of different species. Annie is writing a dissertation about trans girls and play. She loves mermaids.

* * *

"Gulliver Phantasies" was first delivered as an address to a group of psychoanalysts here in New York City. Ferenczi told them, "In your observation of patients you have all come across psychotics who had hallucinations about giants and dwarfs, such hallucinations being accompanied by feelings of anxiety and fear.... Some psychiatrists have given them the name of *Lilliputian* hallucinations." He says that in his experience, such hallucinations or dreams are always somehow connected to early childhood and are again linked to a desire to return to the womb. He gives a couple of interesting case studies from his own practice: a woman who often dreamed of "tiny little black men" that she felt compelled to gobble up like little pieces of poop such that she might transform her whole body into a "male genital" and a man who used to masturbate while fantasizing about having "a little, imaginary, female figure which he always carried in his pocket and from time to time took out and played with." Naturally, that made me remember that silly film with Jean Marais. Ferenczi had another male patient who said that while jerking off, he always imagined himself "a big man, surrounded by a whole harem of tiny women, who served, washed, and caressed him, combed his pubic hair, and then played with his genital until ejaculation ensued" (285–88).

After his discussion of these clinical case studies, Ferenczi says, "I will now try to enliven the monotony of this dry and somewhat theoretical argument by reading some passages from the two first journeys of our friend and colleague, Gulliver, in the hope that perhaps they will make my constructions seem somewhat more probable." That's funny because of course the clinical case studies are anything but dry and also because it seems counterintuitive to offer Gulliver's fantastic travels as ostensibly grounding narratives for a psychoanalytic theory. Ferenczi goes on to recount the episode in which Gulliver is tended to by a gaggle of Lilliputian ladies about the size of his own finger. They're measuring him in order to make him some clothes. "[They] took my measure as I lay on the ground, one standing at my neck, and another at my mid-leg.… Then they measured my right thumb and desired no more; for, by a mathematical computation, that twice round the thumb is once round the wrist, and so on to the neck and waist." Ferenczi points out that it's interesting that the finger, "the typical genital symbol," becomes the standard measure for the whole body (290–91). He also notes the obvious connection between this story and that of his patient's masturbation fantasy. Then he examines a passage among the colossal Brobdingnagians in which a woman tosses her pinky ring around Gulliver's neck, indicating, according to Ferenczi, that "only his head would be big enough to fulfill the sexual task for which normally an organ of the size of a finger suffices" (297). I find it refreshing that Ferenczi, while not a lesbian, recognizes that a finger, or something finger size, might be sexually satisfying. I say, "while not a lesbian," but Ferenczi had no aversion to female homosexuality, which he refused to pathologize. And as you perhaps know, when Ferenczi and Freud first met, there was some awkwardness between them having to do with transference. At one point, Freud wrote a letter to Carl Jung complaining that Ferenczi was "a dear fellow, but dreamy in a disturbing kind of way, and his attitude towards me is infantile. He never stops admiring me, which I don't like, and is probably sharply critical of me in his unconscious when I am taking it easy. He has been too passive and receptive, letting everything be done for him like a woman, and I really haven't got enough homosexuality in me to accept him as one" (353).

But back to the essay. Ferenczi goes on to give a very brief biographical sketch of Jonathan Swift: he was born in Ireland to English parents on November 30, 1667—seven months after the death of his father. His doting nurse kidnapped him as a baby, absconding with him to England. He remained there, in precarious health, for three years. Ferenczi deduces that these unusual circumstances led him to an unresolved castration anxiety. As an adult, Swift developed a series of unusual attachments to women, or girls, which Ferenczi narrates in a somewhat convoluted and probably inaccurate way. There was a little girl named Esther (elsewhere she's called Hester) Johnson, whom Swift had tutored from the age of eight. Swift preferred to call her "Stella." Ferenczi refers to their "famous marriage" in separate abodes, but in fact there's no certainty about that marriage ever taking place. Swift did briefly court, and then scare off, a certain Jane Waring, whom he preferred to call Varina. Swift's older sister was also named Jane. Ferenczi doesn't mention yet another Esther, or Hester, who came later—and whom Swift preferred to call Vanessa. More about all of these later, but suffice it to say, he had a tendency to keep women at arm's length.

In his lecture, Ferenczi didn't really need to belabor the point to the American psychoanalysts: "I think that the biographical argument confirms our supposition that Gulliver fantasies in which persons and objects are magnified or minimized express the sense of genital inadequacy of a person whose sexual activities have been inhibited by intimidation and fixations in childhood." But if it sounds like Ferenczi was belittling Swift, or Gulliver, he ends by apologizing for his own analysis of "Swift and his masterpiece," which "has perhaps been too long," and says he "cannot do better than conclude with a slightly altered quotation from Gulliver himself: 'I hope my readers will excuse me for dwelling on these and similar particulars; however insignificant they may appear, yet they may perhaps help a philosopher to enlarge his thoughts and imagination so that he may apply them to the benefit of public as well as of private life'" (299–300).

I hope you will excuse me for dwelling on these and similar particulars. In fact, I'm going to enlarge them, because Phyllis Greenacre also did.

* * *

I began this story by saying, "I first encountered the work of Phyllis Greenacre while preparing a lecture on D. W. Winnicott." In 2008, Nellie L. Thompson published an article in the *Psychoanalytic Quarterly* that began almost exactly the same way. Dr. Thompson, a psychoanalyst, had run across an obscure reference to Greenacre in a footnote in Winnicott's *Playing and Reality,* the book in which Winnicott lays out his ideas about transitional objects. In that footnote, Winnicott conceded to the influence of Phyllis Greenacre on his thinking in an earlier publication and said, "Unfortunately, I failed to put into the book an acknowledgment of this fact." Dr. Thompson wrote, "I was surprised to learn that Greenacre's work had played any role in Winnicott's thinking and bemused by his admission that he had 'failed' to acknowledge Greenacre's influence. Any influence by Greenacre has received little, if any, recognition." Thompson went on to describe the transatlantic friendship between the British Winnicott and the American Greenacre, arguing that while psychoanalytic history often recounts the "drama" of unsurprisingly Oedipal "rebellion of sons and daughters against the father," it often fails to recognize the gentle and mutual contributions of friends exchanging ideas (252–54).

The story of Winnicott's admitted "failure" to credit Greenacre may sound like a disturbingly familiar story of an unacknowledged female influence, but Thompson also notes that

Winnicott was not much of a believer in what we call intellectual property—his own or that of others. He sort of jokingly referred to "stolen" ideas in his writing, but he also seemed to think that sometimes people have similar ideas at the same time, and it makes little difference who came first, as we all make use of them in different ways. "I am only too happy," he wrote, "when after making my own statement, I find that what I have said has been said previously by others. Often it has been said better, but not better for me" (cited in Thompson, 271). Greenacre herself acknowledged this, though late in life, when Winnicott's widow, Clare, wrote a paper on her husband's use of the terms "the ordinary devoted mother," "the transitional object," and "the facilitating environment," Greenacre scribbled in the margin next to this last term: "taken over from me—PG" (cited in Thompson, 274).

* * *

I often find myself urging my students not to be too proprietary about ideas. About twenty-five years ago I taught a seminar on dance ethnography, and three of the students in it ended up writing dissertations that used the term *social choreography*, which was largely the focus of our discussions, though not a phrase I remember using myself. Each of these students complained to me in private, bitterly, that she had invented the term, and it was stolen by her peers in that seminar. I had no recollection of who, if any of them, had coined the phrase—in fact, I'm quite sure that the figure of coinage is both inaccurate and telling. I think they'd all identify as anticapitalists. Capitalism, I'm sure I don't need to tell you, exerts a particularly brutal and restrictive social choreography. But I do tell my students that it's always good to give a shout-out to anybody who has less visibility than you.

Hm, saying that made me feel self-conscious because I told you about the books that I recommended to my student Annie, but I didn't say much about her own work. I just Googled her scholarship, and I realized there's someone else named Annie Sansonetti who is publishing academic articles — apparently while affiliated with the Sorbonne Université. That Annie cowrote, among other things, "Characteristics of Cervico-Ocular Responses in the Chameleon" and "Spontaneous Saccades under Different Visual Conditions in the Pigeon." My friend and student Annie would love these titles, and they certainly evoke *The Animal Family*, but she didn't write them. She did write "Stage Directions for Trans Girls in Love." She is a romantic, and simply great.

* * *

I really wanted to love *Swift and Carroll: A Psychoanalytic Study of Two Lives.* But in truth, when it finally arrived, I found it somewhat disappointing. Relative to Ferenczi's essay, the book goes into much greater detail on Swift's biography and appears to correct some inaccuracies, and possibly introduce others, but the fundamental psychoanalytic insights seem to me entirely derived from Ferenczi's earlier work. Also, the prose is a little awkward and often redundant. Weirdly, Greenacre makes only one brief mention of Ferenczi, in a footnote on page 261, saying that *he* mentions a previously written (though unpublished) psychoanalytic study of Swift by Hanns Sachs. She doesn't say that Ferenczi had already written her entire thesis in a much more compressed and elegant way.

But maybe, if you go along with Winnicott on these things, it doesn't really matter who got the idea first that Jonathan Swift had unresolved castration anxiety on account of his traumatic early childhood and then expressed it through fantasies of miniature people.

Here, I had to stop and check myself. It's not nothing that she corrected those biographical inaccuracies, and some of the ones she introduces are also of interest. And of course, she extended the argument to the work of Lewis Carroll. But when I went back to the book just now, certain passages jumped out at me that hadn't struck me when I first read them a few months ago: the passages on both Swift's and Carroll's hypochondria and preoccupation with hygiene.

S and I took a COVID-19 test last week and just received our negative results. We had no symptoms and have been taking great pains to avoid infection, particularly in light of S's risk factors. Neither of us is particularly hypochondriacal—in fact, in our fairly long lives, we've both tended to be of the build-up-your-antibodies school. But like everybody else, we've been wavering in the last few months between reasonable caution and outright paranoia.

* * *

Maybe you're wondering what hypochondria and miniaturism have to do with one another—or maybe it's obvious to you that germs are very tiny things, though one's fear of them can be quite overwhelming (even when we identify with them—think here of Raquel Welch in *Fantastic Voyage*). According to Phyllis Greenacre, Jonathan Swift "apparently suffered from severe anxiety and diffuse hypochondriasis of the type which so often accompanies an unusually severe castration complex." He was famously concerned with what he considered to be the inherent "filthiness" of women. "Another characteristic of Swift's hypochondriasis," Greenacre says, "was that it always increased when he was confronted by sickness in others. Then he frequently turned away, in seeming callousness, but generally felt worse himself at once." Greenacre sympathetically offers the possibility that his repulsion by the sickness of others made him feel guilty, though she adds, "there is further the question whether the sight of suffering did not cause him to take it onto himself through a process of primary identification" (92). Maybe these two reactions are actually the same thing.

Lewis Carroll—that is, Charles Dodgson—was similarly afraid of sick people and their infectiousness. Dodgson had a history of respiratory difficulties. An early, severe case of whooping cough permanently compromised his lungs. He was a lifelong germophobe. At one point he received a letter from a child who was convalescing from scarlet fever, and it freaked him out. That would have struck me as unreasonable a few months ago, but that was before I went through my own phase of sanitizing the mail. I've stopped, of course, since they determined that the risk of transmission of COVID-19 through mail and packages is very low. Oops. I just Googled that again and of course found a recently updated medical website that still advises:

Avoid direct contact with the delivery person
    Leave the package outside for a few hours and/or spray it with aerosol disinfectant before handling

Dispose of all outer packaging immediately

Wash your hands thoroughly for 20 seconds or more

Disinfect any high-touch surfaces you had contact with after handling

Avoid touching your face, including your mouth, eyes and nose

I'd stopped the disinfecting part, though I'd kept up all the rest. Maybe I need to reconsider.

Anyway, back to Lewis Carroll—or Dodgson, if you prefer. He had a morbid fear of breathing contaminated air and a gulping appetite for air he considered clean. Greenacre cites Gertrude Chataway, "one of Carroll's little girl friends," who remembered his behavior when they vacationed near each other by the sea: "He would come onto his balcony which joined ours, sniffing the air with his head thrown back and would walk right down the steps on to the beach with his chin in the air, drinking in the fresh breezes as if he could never have enough" (175).

Since the recommendation of near-total confinement here relaxed a bit, S and I have, almost every day, taken a walk to the Hudson River. Carefully maintaining our social distance from the joggers, we make our way to the end of the pier, where we face the setting sun and remove our masks to breathe. S closes his eyes and drinks in the fresh breezes as if he could never have enough. He finds this very helpful. I started following his lead. Actually, I also find it helpful.

* * *

In March, a young colleague of mine who lives in our building told me that she, her husband, and her young baby all appeared to have contracted COVID-19. Their cases were mild, but she asked me to pick up some baby Tylenol and leave it outside her door. I was checking in with her by text and things seemed to be okay, until a few days later when I received a distressing message saying that her father, who had dined with them shortly before their symptoms emerged, had been admitted to a hospital and put on a ventilator. Shortly after that, he died. He was sixty-five and had no other risk factors, unless you count being Latino, which, she later said, she understood to be one, since "in this country, all risk is racialized."

This sent me on a spiral of despair. Of course, we'd been hearing the sirens and reading the figures, and we knew many people were dying in New York, but this felt very close to home—quite literally. In the preceding weeks, S and I had offered to babysit for my colleague's baby every Friday afternoon. Having been a single mother myself at the start of my academic career, I knew that a few hours' break from changing diapers could be very helpful when trying to prepare a class or a manuscript. But the offer was anything but charitable: both S and I were craving a little infantile companionship, and the baby in question was adorable. For a couple of weeks, S cooed at the little guy in French, and I cuddled him and sang him the same lullabies I'd sung to Leo. Then all that kind of thing stopped, and then there was the tragedy. Naturally, our loss of the opportunity to develop a relationship with a kind of surrogate grandchild, as well as my colleague's loss of a little time to get writing done, was minuscule in relation to the terrible loss of her father, who sounded like an extraordinary, vital, and loving man. He was a clinical psychiatrist and an amateur sketch artist and operatic composer. The word she used to describe him was *effervescent*.

It made me very sad and very afraid. That's when I started sanitizing the mail and the groceries.

* * *

Lewis Carroll was probably somewhat anorexic. He ate barely anything, and his sketches often depicted people over- or undereating, and so, correspondingly, either obese or emaciated. An early sketch of his shows a family taking in "homeopathic doses" of food—not even crumbs—and one child asks whether another should have "another molecule" (172). They worry about not being able to see the tiny particles they might be ingesting.

Jonathan Swift loved to eat, but he wasn't without his own food-related neuroses. Greenacre says: "By the age of twenty-two, he was rather frequently complaining of ill-health: weakness, pains, stomach-aches (sometimes physical pains and sometimes figurative statements of aversion), headaches, and rather diffuse body pains. He also developed attacks of dizziness with deafness, thought to be Ménière's disease; but attributed by him to the eating of 'stone fruits.' Many of his complaints had to do with gastrointestinal disturbances" (92).

S also has some original theories about his own gastrointestinal disturbances, though it's true that doctors haven't really been able to offer a more plausible explanation than something like the eating of "stone fruits." He has, to his credit, been eating a few more fruits and vegetables since we started the virtual quarantine.

* * *

I said I'd get back to those women, or girls, in Swift's life. Greenacre parses things out in much greater detail than Ferenczi. Actually, I should really start with that doting nurse. It seems Swift had been a delicate baby, and for some reason, his nurse felt compelled to take him, without his mother's knowledge or permission, to the town of Whitehaven, in England. When his mother found out, she herself said he should stay there until he got stronger. When he was finally returned to her in Ireland, she almost immediately bailed on him. She went back—alone—to Leicester, where she was born, leaving him with his uncle. As for the doting nurse, Greenacre says, Swift "seems to have consigned [her] to anonymity, which was later his way with those who displeased him." He appears, however, to have forgiven his mother when he came to know her as an adult. There's a little anecdote about her trying, one time, to convince Swift's landlady that she was her son's lover. (Greenacre says, parenthetically, "This is cited by one biographer as indicating that he acquired his tendency to practical joking from her" [22–23].)

It was when he was twenty-one, after rejoining his mother in England, that Swift met Esther, or Hester, Johnson, the eight-year-old daughter of a widow. Swift had joined the household of his employer, Sir William Temple, who was also a family friend. Temple was something of a surrogate father figure for Swift. The girl's mother was an acquaintance of the

Temples. Swift tutored Esther (or Hester, or, to him, Stella) for about seven years, before meeting Jane Waring (Varina), the sister of a college friend. He claimed to want to marry Waring but apparently acted a little strangely, and so he wore her out. Greenacre conjectures that this added to his sense of sexual inadequacy. Of the breakup with Waring, Greenacre writes, "On the whole, one's sympathy is with Swift" (34), though Ferenczi had made Varina's bolting sound like the only reasonable decision.

When things didn't work out with Varina, Swift refocused on Stella. Sir William Temple died in 1699, when Swift was thirty-two and Stella was nineteen. While some rumors had circulated that Stella was Temple's illegitimate daughter, that's probably not true. Still, Temple's death seemed to open some possibilities in Swift's mind—or to close some, depending on your perspective. He got a piece of property near Dublin, where he re-created Temple's garden in miniature, and he "persuaded" Stella and her nurse to move there—probably not into his actual house, but nearby. Stella was always in the company of her nurse, Rebecca Dingley. Greenacre says that Dingley "is supposed not to have been in the least infatuated with Swift nor he with her" (39). This "strange triangle" continued for twenty-seven years. It's tempting (to me, at least) to think that Dingley was the lesbian lover of "Stella," but none of Swift's biographers has offered that suggestion. They did, however, note that he addressed Stella as "Young Sir," and told her that neither she nor Dingley was a woman. "Why," he once wrote Stella, "are you not a young fellow, and then I might prefer you?" (40). Which is not exactly the inversion of what Freud wondered about Ferenczi, but it sort of is.

In 1710, Swift began writing *Journal to Stella*, a series of letters that mixed observations on literature and politics with hypochondriacal rants and, in Greenacre's words, "barely decipherable personal communications written in a kind of baby-talk pig Latin." He and Stella called that their "little language" (41). But in that same year (or maybe a little earlier—the accounts vary), Swift met Esther (or Hester) Vanhomrigh, Vanessa, who was about seven years younger than Stella. She was also the daughter of a widow, living in London. For a while, he kept up relations, and correspondences, with both Esthers, one in Ireland, one in England. Vanessa may have been younger, but she apparently acted more like a "woman"—that is, it sounds like she and Swift might actually have been noodling around, which is a foodish metaphor for sex, though the metaphor, or secret code, they used in their correspondence was "drinking coffee" together. He once wrote her, "The best maxim I know in life is to drink your coffee when you can, and when you cannot, to be easy without it.... This much I sympathize with you, that I am not cheerful enough to write, for, I believe, coffee once a week is necessary for that" (44). Evidently, Vanessa had been wanting more coffee.

S and I often gently console each other about the deprivations of this period of isolation and, for him, exile. We notice the little pleasures we have together. Sometimes he'll hold me by the shoulders, stare moonily into my eyes, and say, "And tomorrow morning, we get to drink coffee together."

Neither of the Esthers, or Hesters, was particularly happy about the other's existence. Swift had two other terms of endearment for Vanessa and Stella, respectively: "the brat" and "the agreeable bitch." When Vanessa finally demanded that Swift give up Stella, things came to a head, and he sent Vanessa packing. Vanessa died in 1723 of tuberculosis. Stella died in 1728, and Swift was disconsolate. When he died seventeen years later, he was buried beside her, at his request.

* * *

As I said, Swift met Stella when she was eight. Greenacre says that Alice Liddell was "almost eight," but in fact she was ten years old when she and her sisters (Edith, eight, and Lorina, thirteen) famously took a trip on a rowboat with Charles Dodgson, and Alice asked him to tell them a story. After he did so, Alice told him to write it down, and several months later he gave her the manuscript of *Alice's Adventures under Ground*—later, of course, *Alice's Adventures in Wonderland*.

I probably don't need to say too much about Lewis Carroll's penchant for little girls, which everybody seems to know of. Most people also seem to know that he led a bifurcated existence—as "the meticulous, overexact, boring and probably bored mathematician, the Oxford don, Charles L. Dodgson; and the storyteller of grotesque nonsense fantasy, the famous Lewis Carroll" (126). Greenacre gives glimpses of Carroll's own childhood, his very kissy relationship with his mother, and his jealousy when she turned her attentions to her other children. Once she wrote "Charlie" a letter that closed with "a billion kisses, a gift," Greenacre writes, "which he repaid many times over later in life, when in writing to little girls usually of seven to eleven, he would in turn send them many kisses, often measured and weighed, lest they prove too heavy for proper delivery" (122). Dodgson's mother died when he was nineteen.

He was about thirty when he got close to the Liddell family, but apparently still very kissy, at least with the girls. This may have "set [their] mother on edge," as she seems to have tried to put limits on Dodgson's access to her daughters, and she later destroyed all his letters to Alice (152).

Greenacre says that while Carroll, unlike Swift, never had any romantic attachment to an adult woman, "the child Alice was in some measure a reversed-in-age image of his mother." She bases this theory on the photographs that Carroll took of Alice in "strikingly unchildlike" positions, in a nightgown, with her pre-pubescent chest exposed, and, in one, with the gown drawn up above the knees. "The hands," she writes, "are generally clasped at the waist and the appearance is one of sleep or unconsciousness." They evoke, for Greenacre, "the posture... of a sleeping or dead woman.... [I]t seems that these pictures may represent a fusion of the mother, peaceful after the birth of a child, the nursing mother, and the dead mother. All this is then guarded against or nullified in the little model's being a child" (251).

Weighing Swift's "neurotic confusions" in both his writing and his life ("reversal of sexes, reversal of generations, identification of total body with phallus and vice versa") against Carroll's, she finds the latter "to be closer to the psychotic" (256). She knows she's going out on a limb here. She cites several other critics who had attempted a psychoanalytic reading of Carroll's magnum opus, producing a flurry of outraged responses from *Alice*'s passionate defenders. Greenacre doesn't deny the originality—and indeed the genius—of Carroll's writing.

Greenacre is careful, throughout her book, to say what it's not—neither an aesthetic appreciation of the two men as writers nor a historical contextualization of their work. "Some readers," she acknowledged, "may complain that not enough attention has been paid to the cultural and social influences in the lives of the two men, and that I have confined myself too exclusively to the psychoanalytic approach." She leaves that to "others more competent in these fields than I" (13–14).

Indeed, plenty of other critics took up a more sociological approach to both Swift and Carroll—that is, what's often called new historicism, an attempt to place literary works in their sociopolitical context. Not a few pointed out the Orientalist scene in *Alice* in which she encounters the Caterpillar "quietly smoking a long hookah." *Alice* was published at the height of the British Empire. In 1990, Jon Stratton wrote that the book might be read as "a fantasy of civilising the natives" (170). But in that scene, it's the Caterpillar who imperiously tells Alice: "Explain yourself!" She doesn't do a very good job of it, as her own shapeshifting has addled her: "being so many different sizes in a day is very confusing." The Caterpillar rejects this, but she tells him that when he turns into a chrysalis—"you will some day, you know—and then after that into a butterfly"—he'll surely feel "a little queer" himself. He doubts it, but she says, "all I know is, it would feel very queer to me." "'You!' said the Caterpillar contemptuously. 'Who are *you*?'" (58–61).

That's what Breton asked Nadja, though apparently not contemptuously.

At least three adaptations of the story of *Alice's Adventures in Wonderland* have been made in which Alice is Black or Brown. Erin Taylor published one version in 2019, in which Alice is African. Whoopi Goldberg wrote one in 1992, in which she's African American (that one takes place in New

York City). And, in 1975, Nanci Sheppard and Donna Leslie published one in which Alice is renamed Alitji, and she's Aboriginal Australian. That was a bilingual edition in English and Pitjantjatjara.

When it comes to Swift, sociopolitical readings abound. Also in 1990, Laura Brown published "Reading Race and Gender: Jonathan Swift," saying that "the works of Jonathan Swift provide a test case for political criticism and a proving ground for the nature of the 'politics' of such a criticism." Brown calls Swift "an explicit misogynist and also an explicit anti-colonialist." She says this poses a problem for a feminist, anticolonialist critic: "Which [Swift] to choose? What is a marxist/feminist to do?" (425–26). She points to the passage where Gulliver sticks herbs in his nose to avoid his wife's womanly stink. Brown flails a bit in a few other eighteenth-century texts to find places where other writers associate womanliness with what really stinks: "mercantile capitalism" and particularly the commodities generated through colonial exploitation. You might find that a bit of a stretch.

S never tells me that I smell bad, but he does have an exquisite olfactory sense. Seriously, he can smell a cigarette or a ripe fruit or a piece of poop from a mile away. This has been occasionally reassuring since they determined that anosmia was a common symptom of COVID-19.

Brown does turn to some interesting passages in Swift where he either recuperates an image of femininity or places Gulliver in what she considers to be a feminized role—maybe most charmingly in the bit in book 4 when he horses around with some Brobdingnagian gals: "The handsomest among these maids of honor, a pleasant frolicsome girl of sixteen, would sometimes set me astride upon one of her nipples, with many other tricks, wherin the reader will excuse me for not being over particular" (cited in Brown, 343).

S is also pretty discreet about such things, so I won't make any connections here to our own nipple play.

In 2006, Elaine Robinson published *Gulliver as Slave Trader: Racism Reviled*, probably the most extreme of the celebrations of Swift's race politics, which she considered to still have "disturbing relevance" in the twenty-first century. Robinson argues that Gulliver represents a slave trader and that Swift's book is a brutal, if satirical, condemnation of white supremacism. Again, some of her evidence might appear to be a stretch—such as her reading of the fictional name "Lilliput" as "a protest in itself: [against] Lily-white men launching [i.e., putting] ships across the oceans to capture innocent black human beings to forcefully carry across an ocean" (41). It seems to me the problem with that sentence isn't so much its exegetical argument as the redundancy of Robinson's prose. Maybe that sounds like nit-picking, but nit-picking, let's face it, is itself a Lilliputian sort of activity.

One reviewer, Richard Terry of Northumbria University, took Elaine Robinson to task for hazarding that reading of "Lilliput." But he said, "What seems most questionable, however, is that Swift's motivation in depicting Gulliver in such repugnant terms is to foster 'white self-hatred,' an attitude that Ms. Robinson sees as being both justified and to be encouraged" (67). He also misidentified Robinson as "Eleanor" in his review. I hesitated to make Professor Terry sound, himself, persnickety, and I looked him up, and now I feel even stranger about noting his error. It seems he died just a few weeks ago, after a brief illness. There's no indication that this was COVID-19. In looking for his obituary, I found there was another Richard Terry who died around the same time, but he was from a suburb of Flint, Michigan. The two Richards seem to have been of roughly the same age. Flint is about half an hour from Pontiac, Michigan, which is where my mother was born. The Richard Terry from Michigan spent his life working for McDonald's—in fact, his obituary says: "The family would like to thank the McDonald's family for all of their love and support during these unprecedented times." There's also no indication whether he died of COVID-19. He was five years older than me and four years younger than S. He was the age of my colleague's father.

* * *

Phyllis Greenacre was particularly aware of the fanaticism of Lewis Carroll's devotees, but there have long been and still are plenty of people ardently defending Jonathan Swift from the tides, feminist and otherwise. Actually, even the people who hated him helped to secure his place in literary history. In Swift's own century, Laetitia Pilkington's *Memoirs* recorded many of the biographical details that would be spun out over the years. Pilkington, who knew him socially, makes all kinds of excuses for his odd behavior, which included an episode, relayed by Virginia Woolf in her introduction to Pilkington's text, in which Swift slammed Pilkington against a wall so he could "measure" her. His calculation: three feet, two inches. Laetitia supposedly complained that it was his hand pushing down on her head that made her shrink to half her size, but, Woolf writes, "she was foolish to complain. Probably she owed her intimacy to that very fact, she was only three feet two. Swift had lived a lifetime among the giants; now there was a charm in dwarfs. He took the little creature into his library" (Woolf). That's probably apocryphal. Anyway, after Pilkington divorced her philandering, sadistic husband (she was also caught *in flagrante* with somebody, but that's another story), Swift damned her "as the most profligate whore in either kingdom"—English or Irish ("Laetitia Pilkington"). Still, she maintained that it was Swift who taught her how to write.

In nineteenth-century England, even though the political tides turned against him, Swift remained a major literary preoccupation of those who opposed his views (whatever they were—hard to pin down in any satirist, but especially this one). William Makepeace Thackeray really nailed him in *The English Humorists of the Eighteenth Century*, but that contributed to his continued visibility as much as anything else. That kind of thing continued through the early and mid-twentieth century, but Swift had his rabid defenders, many women, including Mary M. Colum and later Kathleen Williams. I find it both touching and a little disturbing that it's often women who were his apologists.

In 2017, the *Times Literary Supplement* published a review by Claude Rawson of the two most recent Swift biographies: Eugene Hammond's two-volume *Jonathan Swift: Irish Blow-In* and *Jonathan Swift: Our Dean* (2016) and John Stubbs's *Jonathan Swift: The Reluctant Rebel* (2017). According to Rawson, the former wants Swift "to conform to current notions of political virtue, resembling a liberal campus chaplain (or Desmond Tutu or Martin Luther King . . .)." Rawson claims that "this sanitizing of Swift" has been going on since the 1950s and 1960s (Rawson). Sanitizing is an interesting metaphor. Hammond apparently extends the "sanitizing" to his account of Swift's attitudes toward sex and sexuality, saying he had "playfully relaxed heterosexual inclinations" and a "lifelong comfort with women of all ages and social classes." Hm. Rawson finds Stubbs a bit subtler, and he also prefers his prose. He's befuddled by some of Hammond's chapter titles (e.g., "Everybody Poops") and by his "gratuitous and embarrassing decision to call Swift's two principal women friends Hetty and Hessy" (the Esthers, or Hesters, or, if you will, Stella and Vanessa). Sorry to get all psychoanalytic about it, but that sounds a bit like repetition compulsion. Then again, I haven't read the book. Hammond's, I mean.

* * *

It's true that "Everybody Poops" seems like a weird title for a chapter in a two-volume biography of Swift. But who am I to talk? Just yesterday I received a copy of Kathleen Meyer's *How to Shit in the Woods*, which I'd ordered for possible inclusion on the syllabus of a course I'll start teaching (online) in the fall. The course is called the *Performance of Everyday Life*, and the first text on the syllabus is Michel de Montaigne's beautiful essay "Of Experience," in which he goes into meticulous detail about how, where, and when he likes to do certain things, such as having breakfast, having sex, and taking a shit. The first two are things S and I do together, so we know each other's inclinations. We don't really keep tabs on each other's defecation preferences. He did tell me, though, that when he first moved to the country, one of his great pleasures was peeing outside at night, in the garden, under the stars.

the handwriting on the wall

....

I recently submitted a sample of my handwriting to an on-line graphologist, and I received the following report:

> To begin the analysis, the first aspect of the handwriting to consider is the flow. Some handwriting is rigid and taut, as if the forward movement of the pen has been restrained, while other script has great flow, fluency and vitality. This handwriting adopts the middle line between these two extremes. The subject has carefully maintained a style which achieves a middle ground between complete freedom and total control. This reflects a desire to avoid extremes, and it is also likely to reveal itself in other aspects of her life. She may tend to adopt either a controlled and conformist attitude or, equally, may choose to follow a freer, less conformist lifestyle. Which course is adopted will very much depend on the circumstances at the time, and is never likely to be as extreme as would be found in individuals with fully restrained or released script. Thus, the subject is flexible and adaptable to the demands of a particular situation in a way that other types of writers would find almost impossible.

The pressure used throughout the script is average in intensity, indicating that the subject is able to maintain a balance between too much activity and too great a degree of lethargy. As a result, she lacks the intense drive and enthusiasm shown by writers with heavy pressure, but will be equally tolerant of inactivity in those who use a lower pressure in their script. She will be good at working methodically at the more routine tasks. The habitual use of black ink indicates a strong attitude towards communication. The subject is concerned with precision, exactitude and in the clear understanding of all aspects of the message she is trying to convey. She has a strong desire to make herself clear and to avoid confusions. Frequently the habitual use of black ink is associated with people in professions which demand a high degree of precision, such as accountancy, engineering, mathematics and such.

A number of artful simplifications in the handwriting show that the subject is considerably intelligent (scoring 3 out of a possible 5 in the IQ categories). She has the intellectual capacity that would enable her to be successful in a career such as teaching, journalism or computer programming.
None of this came as a surprise.

* * *

I often write letters by hand and send them through the mail. This doesn't mean I don't use email—in fact, I send plenty of emails, too, but I love letters. That bit about "black ink" in my handwriting analysis is actually a little off. It's true that if I use a pen, it's usually one with black ink, but my stylus of preference is the pencil because I like to be able to erase things. I suppose this still counts as evidence of a "desire to make [myself] clear and to avoid confusions," but it also evidences my tendency to change my mind. And maybe to create confusion. Sometimes, instead of erasing, I purposefully cross something out in order to register my own rethinking things or even my own accidents. Although my writing's quite clear, I occasionally, also purposefully, write a word a little messily such that it might be construed two ways, both of which interest me. I feel a little guilty when I fudge things like that, but not very. Anyway, these are some of the reasons I still send letters through the post.

I also like the possibility of enclosing things in the envelope, like dried flowers or tiny gifts. In the course I taught in the spring, online, I asked all my students for their mailing addresses, and I sent them postcard reproductions of the postcard that Jacques Derrida wrote about in *La carte postale*, with a Matthew Paris image of Plato and Socrates, in which the student appears to be guiding the writing of the teacher. When the course was over, I wrote them all letters about their work, and I enclosed little hand sanitizer cozies that I'd knitted for them, just big enough to hold a tiny plastic bottle. I told them when the pandemic was over, they could use them to carry some more cheerful product, like DIY massage oil or personal lubricant. I gave them an excellent recipe for the latter (boil down two and a half tablespoons of flaxseeds in two cups of water and strain). Don't worry, they were all graduate students, so I don't think they were shocked. This is perhaps another piece of evidence that I "may tend to adopt either a controlled and conformist attitude or, equally, may choose to follow a freer, less conformist lifestyle." Indeed, this depends on the circumstances at the time.

Micrographia is the technical term for abnormally small handwriting, and while it's sometimes associated with certain personality traits, it's also associated with certain neurological disorders, such as those that occur in patients with Parkinson's disease, or people with other kinds of brain lesions. But some people do it with intention. One of the better-known writers who purposefully employed micrographia was Robert Walser, whom I love. A few years ago, my best friend and I read *The Assistant* together, and later she gave me a copy of Walser's *Microscripts*. The latter was published in English in 2012, translated and with an introduction by Susan Bernofsky. The manuscripts of these pieces were, as this edition tells you, "narrow strips of paper, covered with tiny ant-like pencil markings a millimeter high, [which] came to light only after the author's death in 1956. At first considered random restless pencil markings or a secret code, the microscripts were in time discovered to be a radically miniaturized form of antique German script: a whole story was deciphered on the back of a business card" (book jacket).

One might say that all of Walser's writing is diminutive in the sense that it evokes an aesthetic of understatement, modesty, and self-effacement — even as these qualities reveal a certain underlying monstrosity. Is he ironic? Yes and no. It's the stylistic equivalent of leaving a word illegible such that it might make two meanings possible at once. That's pretty sneaky, and it could be the trick of a rascally schoolboy. Many of Walser's stories take place in an educational setting. Students defer, with exaggerated docility, to their teachers — but that docility only undermines the reader's sense of the author-ity of the instructor.

You may be thinking that I try to circumvent this sort of thing with my own students by undermining my own au-thority, like when I sent them those Matthew Paris postcards. That's probably right.

Many critics have noted the way in which Robert Walser's prose seems to erase itself. W. G. Sebald said it "has this ten-dency to dissolve upon reading." Ben Lerner ties this to the temporality of the narration: "Walser is often less concerned with recording the finished thought than with capturing the movement of a mind in the act of thinking." But the erasure, and the diminutiveness, was also literal. Walser developed his "pencil system" in the 1920s and began creating his minitexts on bits of paper—envelopes, receipts, telegrams, calendar pages, and the torn-off covers of pulp fiction (a genre he ap-preciated, as do I). Sometimes he cut these scraps into even smaller pieces. As Bernofsky says, when they were discovered, people assumed they were impossible cryptograms or simply random scribbles. But an old friend of his finally magnified and published a few, and somebody got an inkling that they might be decipherable. I wrote inkling and then stared at it, wondering if it comes from the word ink. Then I looked it up—in fact, it comes from the Middle English verb *inklen*, to whisper. The friend who kept the microscript manuscripts was very protective of them. Only after the friend died, in 1962, were scholars able to begin decoding them, and it took them years. Of course, a few of the decipherings are questionable.

In 1927, Walser wrote a letter to an editor in which he spoke of himself in the third person:

The writer of these lines experienced a time when he hideously, frightfully hated his pen, I can't begin to tell you how sick of it he was; he became an outright idiot the moment he made the least use of it; and to free himself from this pen malaise he began to pencil-sketch, to scribble, fiddle about. With the aid of my pencil I was better able to play, to write; it seemed this revived my writerly enthusiasm. I can assure you (this all began in Berlin) I suffered a real breakdown in my hand on account of the pen, a sort of cramp from whose clutches I slowly, laboriously freed myself by means of the pencil. A swoon, a cramp, a stupor—these are always both physical and mental. So I experienced a period of disruption that was mirrored, as it were, in my handwriting and its disintegration, and when I copied out the texts from this pencil assignment, I learned again, like a little boy, to write. (*Microscripts*, 12)

S often stops to jot things down on random scraps of paper, which he later copies over into a small Clairefontaine notebook. But he's not particular about his stylus or ink. I'm the one that prefers pencil.

* * *

Zachary Schoenhut wrote me back! Their email came yesterday, and they're fine. They'd dawdled in answering my message because they were busy completing their thesis for the Dutch Art Institute, which they attached to their message. The title of Zachary's thesis is "transcribbling: queer acts of archival disruption," and I found it excellent. In the introduction, Zachary notes: "According to etymonline.com, it was noted down somewhere in 1746 that when a transcription was done poorly, it was called *transcribble*" (6). This is the kind of citation that S finds demoralizing, relying as it does on a perhaps not entirely reliable internet trail. As you may have noticed, I indulge in some such citations myself—and tend to push them even further. In fact, I spent quite a bit of time going down the rabbit hole (hello, Alice) of the word *transcribble*. It may not surprise you to learn that there is a cartoon blog by someone named Bridgy Art on webtoons.com called Transcribbles, with the following description: "A sort of diary, sort of story telling device I use to document stuff in my life as a transgender woman." There's also a voice-memo-to-text conversion app called Transcribble, created by a high school student who edits their school newspaper. This student says on their website: "Accomplishments that I'm proud of: I'm very proud of being able to learn to use an app extension and using the speech to text framework" ("Transcribble"). Bridgy's website is notably less self-congratulatory. Her first entry on the blog is "Dysthymia," and the voice inside her head is saying, "Having a bad day, are we? Good. We all know you deserve bad Days you Disgusting freak" ("Transcribbles").

Zachary's thesis opens with a theoretical overview of what they hope *transcribbling* might accomplish—the appropriate (an)archiving of "insurrectionary minoritarian performances, gestures and sounds that communicate through a language of refusal, disrupting procedures of power through modes of imperceptibility and opacity" (5). That is, the thesis considers performances by queer-identified people of color, and it attempts to document them in a language that will, like the performances themselves, resist fixity and reductionism. Three chapters follow: one on a sexual health clinic in Brussels, where a charismatic figure given the fictional name of Major resists "the whiteness that is the medical space" through vogueing gestures; one on the "*snap*" of Black gay men registered in the cinematic work of Marlon Riggs and others; and one on clapping in the time of COVID-19 as an amplification of "rebellious resonance across time and space, echoing from the beginnings of the Civil Rights movement of the US in the 1950s and ricocheting off and to the 2020 Black Trans Lives Matter protest in Brooklyn, as well as in Black Lives Matter protests across the globe" (12–13). My little summary of Zachary's project is, of course, reductive, and it fixates both the subject matter and stylistic interventions. Their thesis ends with a "con-clue-sion": "Nothing is concluding here, to attempt to do so would be to invalidate exactly what *transcribbling* remains open to: clues that shimmer and sparkle against the sky" (57).

The email to which the thesis was attached was very warm. Zachary responded sympathetically to S's and my sadness at not being able to get back to Normandy. Zachary, too, wondered about when and how they'd be able to move. "Prospects for my return to the US seem quite limited at the moment." Fortunately, they share my luck of having good company: a partner named Olivier, with whom they collaborate on both art and life. Also, "Olivier and I are sort of amateur naturalists ourselves." Regarding my writing, they said, "I would love to know more about this toy piano project or maybe not know more about it, but read it at some point." They said a bit more about the possible connection to the Schoenhut company. Although they knew of no direct evidence, "I believe the person who started it has the name Albert Frederick and my father's name is Frederick and Albert pops up somewhere in my family tree…. On another note, I was obsessed with miniature dolls as a child, collected many many miniature figurines and created my own miniature dolls at camp and such. I used to collect these ceramic trinkets found in the Red Rose tea boxes. I could probably write to you more about the little figurines or send you pictures of some of them. Maybe have my mother send you my collection somehow."

They then gave me the email address for Risa Horn. It turns out it is the most obvious one you could imagine. I could easily have guessed it. Maybe that's why she was so coy on her website: she was hiding in full view.

I'd never heard about the Red Rose figurines. I ordered three of them on eBay. I told Zachary I'd hold onto them until we met again in person, when I'd give them to them. I said I didn't know when that would happen, but I felt sure it would.

* * *

After we'd known each other for a couple of years, S told me he had a confession to make. He looked sheepish. He led me into the bedroom and closed the door. Behind it was an area on the painted dark red wall where there was a small rash of little poke marks revealing the white paint underneath. He explained that early in our relationship, each time he'd come to visit, he'd fall into despair on the day of his departure, and he'd take a sharp object and stab the wall there, like a prisoner who makes marks on his cell wall to mark time. But in this case, he was marking his difficult departures.

He kept this up, even when it became clear that he'd be spending more time here than in France. That was a relief to

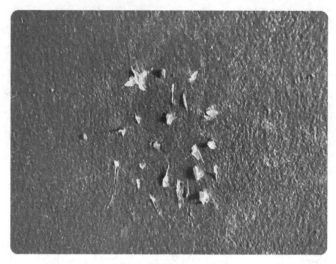

fig 6.1 Stabbed Wall (B. Browning)

---

him at first, though now that he can't get back to his country and his daughters, the figure of a prison cell feels sadly apt. Though of course also not. When I tried to give S some context for the BLM protests, he was astonished to learn about the privatization of US prisons and the capitalizing on mass incarceration. I assured him that many Americans were also unaware of this, even though Angela Davis had been talking about it for a very long time.

When S made those stab marks behind the door, he was writing on the wall. The image of a prisoner in a cell also makes me think of those Argentine dissident women.

* * *

Many people have made a connection between the personal quirks and writerly aesthetics of Robert Walser and Emily Dickinson—including the way they put things on paper. There was a show at the Drawing Center in New York in 2013 that juxtaposed their manuscripts. The curator, Claire Gilman, wrote:

> Although Walser, who was born shortly before Dickinson died, was most likely unaware of her work, both writers were obsessively private as well as peculiarly attentive to the visuality of their texts. Walser wrote in tiny, inscrutable script on narrow strips of paper using an antiquated German alphabet that was long considered indecipherable.... Similarly, Dickinson fitted her multifarious poetic fragments to carefully torn pieces of envelope or stationery, which were discovered among her posthumous papers. (Gilman)

Dickinson's handwriting was not exactly tiny, but she liked scraps of paper, and even when she used regular sheets of paper, she bound her handwritten poems in "fascicles"—little booklets which she "stabbed" with two holes and sewed together.

In biology, a *fasciculus* refers to a bundle of structures, such as nerve or muscle fibers or conducting vessels in plants. *Fasciculus* is the diminutive of the Latin *fascis,* which is also the root of the word fascism.

A graphologist claiming to "know basically nothing about Emily Dickinson's life" wrote a blog post with the following analysis of Dickinson's handwriting:

> The rightward slant of Dickinson's handwriting shows that she is emotionally expressive. She is likely more heart-ruled

than head-ruled. She often relies more on her desires rather than data or pure judgment. She is affectionate and sympathetic, expressing what she feels.

Dickinson's "t"-bars are very long; this is a highly valuable trait that indicates enthusiasm and drive.... Her t-bars are also slanted downwards. People with this trait tend to be good leaders and enjoy being in command. This is the trait of dominance....

Notice that she crosses her "t"s very high on the stem, usually at the very top or even above the stem so that the bar floats by itself. The height plus the length of her "t"-bars indicate that she is a "dreamer," that is, someone whose goals are extremely high and she can literally see herself reaching them. She is a visionary. Along with high goals comes high self-esteem as well: Dickinson has much self-respect and healthy personal boundaries....

Dickinson often leaves large spaces in between her words. This indicates a need for personal space. She may be caring and expressive, but she also needs her space and probably some alone time as well. Give her some room.

Similarly, Dickinson has an independent nature, as shown by her "y"s which often go straight down below the baseline and do not curve upward again. She prefers not to need other people all the time, but rather to get the job done on her own. (*My Strength and My Song*, emphasis in original)

"Healthy personal boundaries" isn't exactly the way Dickinson is popularly perceived, though her "need for personal space" has often been observed, and even invoked in this period of social distancing.

The old "nun of Amherst" version of her story has gotten revised over the years. The two recent biopics of her both emphasize her possible, if not probable, woman-loving nature, but they construe it somewhat differently. The one by an avowedly celibate man who says he "always hated being gay" depicts her as, yes, a lesbian, but profoundly repressed. The one by a fierce queer-identified activist woman has her rolling around in sensual abandon with her sister-in-law. Obviously, we all make of her what we need her to be. I once wrote a novel in which I depicted myself as a YouTube ballerina who cribbed all her own comments from Dickinson's poetry (almost nobody noticed this—Dickinson's poems, with their weird syntax and signature dashes, can really sound like some of the wackadoodle comments you read on YouTube). In my novel, Emily/I seemed pretty "controlled" but turned out to have "follow[ed] a freer, less conformist lifestyle." So why did I feel the need to crib my own lines from Dickinson? Let's face it, she was a visionary. I think it's fair to say she'd probably score higher than three out of a possible five in the IQ categories.

* * *

When S began to despair of ever getting back to the house in Normandy, something occurred to me that I'm quite sure I wouldn't have considered or even thought of under "normal" circumstances. When my mother died, both my sister and I were surprised to learn just how much money she'd managed to squirrel away, and despite her lifelong philosophy of insisting on everybody's financial self-reliance, she'd left us each an unexpected chunk of change. Since I, like her, had been planning for my old age and living pretty frugally—and happily so—this windfall was a little confusing. Though neither my mother nor I was religious, we both tithed—not to any church, of course, but to the various predictable causes that corresponded to both of our preoccupations, some of which overlapped, some of which were different. So, with the part of my inheritance that was liquid, I did that, and then I told my son I'd like to give him half of the rest, but that I'd like him to think carefully about what to do with it. Perhaps I would have made this move on my own, but I was also influenced by something that S had told me about his mother: as she got older, she offered him some of her own savings, telling him she preferred to give him help *la main chaude*—with "the warm hand," that is, while she was still alive. S tended to deflect these offers because, while he could use the help, there was no telling how long his mother would live, and she might need the money herself.

In my case, I felt pretty confident that I'd socked away enough for a rainy day, actually a lot of rainy days, and I figured now was the time when Leo could use it. I explained that to him. He was working for an arts organization at the time, for a fairly measly salary without much promise of advancement, and he'd begun to despair of the corporate vibe there (despite the organization's ostensibly artistic mission). Mostly, he was preparing spreadsheets and PowerPoint presentations. He was paying me a nominal rent for part of our apartment. His space had a separate entrance, and we blocked off the doorway connecting it to my living space with a bookshelf. That meant he effectively had a tiny studio next door, with no kitchen, and S and I were sharing something like a small one-bedroom. It was, for Manhattan, an enviable situation. Still,

Leo felt cramped, not just in terms of square footage, but by the entire situation: trapped in his childhood home, in a frustrating job, and with his imbalanced and occasionally upsetting father clamoring for attention. So, the offer felt to him something like a lifeline. He took seriously my request for him to "think carefully" about what to do with this money. Seriously, but also comically. Using the questionable skill set he'd acquired at work, he made up some spreadsheets and an elaborate PowerPoint presentation with three alternative plans, taking into account various possible glitches. It was mostly realistic but at moments resembled an episode of *Monty Python's Flying Circus*. We agreed that he should go with the moderate plan. I'll spare you the details, but they involved the acquisition of a plane ticket, some photography equipment, and a used van, and culminated in Portland, as you know.

I missed having him as a next-door neighbor, but in truth, we'd tried to give each other a lot of privacy while he was in New York. After my son left, S took to working at "Leo's house" during the day, which was helpful since we both work mostly at home. The nominal rent that Leo had been paying wasn't really a necessity for our getting by. All that to say, even after passing that chunk off with a warm hand, I still had another little chunk in the bank, as well as an annuity account still untouched. I was advised to keep it where my mother had it for a while, so as not to get a whopping tax bill.

For several years, S and I had been largely spending our time together in the New York apartment, as you know, but taking respites in the little shack in Normandy when we could. For me, it was a fairly late-in-life discovery, how sustaining that could be, but for S it had long been a necessity. As I said, the main impetus for his going back to France was to see his daughters. But once he was really stuck here, it became clear that if he didn't get a little fresh air he was going to go downhill very fast. Years before, early in our relationship, he'd written a song called "House in the Country," and it became part of our repertoire. It was a fantasy—"let's buy an ass or a donkey … let's get a goose or a monkey … let's have a home without a key"—but in truth, we were sort of living the fantasy already, until now, because we couldn't get back to Normandy.

We went to visit a friend living in upstate New York (with all the awkward masking and social distancing required for such a visit), and this friend casually observed that he'd bought his house—on a big piece of land where he and his family lived with two horses, two pigs, a goat, a ferret, and sundry other critters—for the price of a cramped one-bedroom in Queens. S and I looked at each other. We didn't need anything that big, but we wondered if we might find some sort of cottage to escape to, even provisionally.

We weren't the only ones with this idea. Just as we began to look into the possibilities, the *New York Times* ran a story about people like us scrambling north of the city. Needless to say, the comments section on this article didn't cast any of us in a particularly flattering light. This was all perplexing, but when I looked at S in despair, all I could think of was how much relief he'd felt when we'd gotten to the country. I wrote a real estate agent a description of us: two writers, American and French, fifty-eight and sixty-eight, with minimal needs, just enough space to work together, in a rural place. We rented a car and met her, and the first place she showed us looked like heaven: a tiny peach-colored house hidden in the woods, on a little road that didn't even get postal delivery. It was next to a nature preserve. We saw a deer as we pulled up. It seemed like a good omen. Miraculously, we found that if I moved around my resources, we could make the down payment. If I rented out "Leo's house" at a just slightly higher rate than that nominal one he'd been paying, I could make the mortgage payments. S said he'd pay for an old clunker with four-wheel drive. We took the plunge.

I told Leo I'd be renting out "his space," and he took it in stride, though he admitted that in moments of despair or anxiety (when the piano store closed, for example), he'd been comforted to think that he had a place to crash if everything went to hell. But he also knew that moving back to his childhood home would have its own psychological repercussions, so this was probably for the best. I thought I'd feel most comfortable with the arrangement if I could find a student who would benefit from the very cheap rent. I sent out some feelers to my "feminist club"—the group of graduate students and artists with whom I work on an editorial collective—but they all had fixed living arrangements, precarious as they were. I posted a notice and a very polite young law student answered, as did another guy, slightly rougher around the edges of his emails, who said he was in the ROTC. I reported these inquiries to S, saying that the law student seemed like an affable person, and I appreciated the gentility of his communications. I said I'd hoped for an arts student, preferably a feminist (for all the obvious reasons), but when I told the law student that there was an upright piano in the space, belonging to my son, he said he had some desire to learn to play, and it seemed perfectly possible, if not probable, that he was a feminist!

As I was giving S little updates about my exchanges with potential renters, he seemed to be confusingly testy about the things I told him. When I was less than enthusiastic about the reserve officer in training, he thought I was being classist (very possibly true, though in my mind I was being a pacifist), and he had a similar response when I praised the elegance of the law student's emails. But there was something more—his testiness just increased when I said the guy wanted to learn to play piano. I'd found that encouraging—S, no. At one point we got into a bit of a tiff—I told him he was increasing the pressure in an already stressful situation by appearing to judge my every move.

The next morning, he more or less confessed to having been unreasonable, but he had an explanation. He told me he'd had a dream which clarified everything. In the dream, he was in his own childhood home, his parents' apartment on the Rue de la Folie Méricourt in Paris. Leo was with him there, and he was informing S that he was taking over S's bedroom so S would have to move out. While you might think such a dream would provoke at least temporary disgruntlement with Leo, in fact it illuminated to S what had been bothering him so much about the law student. He said that the entire scenario reminded him of the most devastating scene in *A Clockwork Orange*. Well, it's odd to say this is the most devastating scene in that film—but that's how S remembers it. It's when the antihero Alex tries to go back to his parents' home but finds his room's been taken over by a "lodger" named Joe who now considers himself a foster son to Alex's parents. "So you're back, eh?" Joe asks him. "You're back to make life a misery for your lovely parents once more, is that it?" They've already gotten rid of all his stuff.

There's no going home. The parents are a little sheepish, yet they're clearly more satisfied with their surrogate son.

S said he couldn't help thinking of that law student as Joe—though of course Leo doesn't resemble Alex at all, except for his rakish good looks, fashion sense, and love of classical music. But, indeed, the law student did come off as something of a "perfect son." I appreciated S taking responsibility for his own projections, which obviously had as much to do with his own childhood as anything else. But I also thought he might have a point. Fortunately, there was one other interested renter—a young woman working toward an MFA in creative writing. I Googled her and noted that her writing—both fiction and nonfiction—took up questions of gender relations and politics with a mix of sensitivity and humor. There wasn't a lot to read yet online—but enough to give you this impression. When I offered her the place, I told her I'd produced three novels there and hoped she'd find it a similarly stimulating place to write. I refrained from making a joke about her being my "mini-me." In fact, when she came to see the place, she fairly towered above me. She was very nice. S seemed relieved.

I don't think Leo would be bothered by my calling Yve my "number two son," but maybe partly because number two is not number one. I just remembered that when Leo spoke about having a child one day, he called that hypothetical person his "tiny me." As you'll recall, he hoped that might be what would finally get Tony off his back.

* * *

As I said, micrographia is the technical term for tiny handwriting, whether it's a result of a physical pathology or an intention. But it can also be an act of craft and dexterity that overcompensates for a disability. Perhaps the most astonishing example is that of Matthias Buchinger, who was born in Germany, in 1674, with phocomelia. Phocomelia, in the mid-twentieth century, was typically associated with the use of thalidomide by pregnant women, but it existed before that, and it can have genetic origins. Etymologically, phocomelia means *having seal limbs.* Buchinger was born without hands or lower legs. His adult height was twenty-nine inches. He lived to the age of sixty-five and had fourteen (acknowledged) children with eight different women, four of whom he'd married (sequentially). He was an itinerant artist and performer, playing various musical instruments, performing magic tricks and other sleights of hand—but he was best known for his illustrations, which he sold. They were minute designs in which parts of the figures, such as locks of hair or branches of plants, were made up of tiny written language. The text was often taken from the Bible. From a distance, you couldn't even see that it was "handwriting." Though Buchinger didn't actually have hands, observers of his craft said he had "growths and callouses" at the end of his upper limbs that he used to grasp a pen. He could also shoot a gun.

Buchinger's own self-assessment, at least publicly, went far beyond the pride of that high school newspaper editor and app developer in their "accomplishments"—to say nothing of the self-doubt expressed by the transwoman cartoonist-transcribbler. Buchinger wrote to one of his patrons: "I do believe there never was a person born without Hands or Feet that can do what I can and is likely there may never be another" (cited in Morse).

Actually, there was somebody who could do something similar, if not exactly the same. Her name was Sarah Biffen (or Biffin, or Beffin), and she was born in England about a century after Buchinger, also with phocomelia. She, like him, was a highly skilled illustrator. She specialized not in micrography but miniature portraiture on ivory. She also sewed.

For a time, during their careers, both Matthias Buchinger and Sarah Biffen enjoyed some fame, and even a little financial security. Charles Dickens mentioned Biffen in more than one novel. But by the ends of their lives, their publics seemed to have gotten a little bored with their acts. Biffen tried to make a comeback as "Mrs. Wright." Maybe she was banking on people's prurient imaginations about her married life. Buchinger also seemed to play on that, and more. If you trust the hearsay on Wikipedia, his reproductive activities may even have surpassed the officially acknowledged fourteen children: he was "rumored to have had children by as many as 70 mistresses" ("Matthias Buchinger"). They also say that "'Buckinger's boot' existed in England as a euphemism for the vagina (because the only 'limb' he had was his penis)." Well, I tracked down the source given in the footnote for that one (*A Classical Dictionary of the Vulgar Tongue*, by Francis Grose, Esq., 1788), and saw that the Wiki author of Buchinger's page had done a bit of elaboration on the dictionary entry. *Buckinger's boot* is defined there as "the monosyllable" — presumably the cunt, which indeed might be rendered "the vagina," but the bit about his "only 'limb'" is an editorial embellishment, or an extended metaphor, depending on how you look at it.

Buchinger had other limbs, and he used one to write. It would have been an even more astonishing feat if he'd done his micrographic illustrations with his penis—he didn't, but it seems to me this image is evoked by the Wiki author's configuration of things. Sarah Biffen used her mouth. *Mouth* is also a monosyllable, and for some, it might bear a figural relationship to "Buckinger's boot." Unlike Buchinger, Biffen didn't create her figures out of writing—they were simply figurative. But I have a feeling that if Buchinger were to hold something over Biffen, it would be that she resorted to using her mouth to make her artwork—and maybe that she wasn't as impressively miniature as he was. Holding something over her, of course, is a figure of speech. Another one would be that Buchinger might feel he had the upper hand. If they'd lived in the same century, Sarah Biffen would have towered over Buchinger, just like my mini-me towered over me. Sarah Biffen was thirty-seven inches tall.

A few years ago, I offered S a sentimental gift, which he wears, constantly, on a chain around his neck. It's a grain of rice with our names written on either side, enclosed in a tiny glass vial filled with liquid. I ordered it online—as you can imagine, that's something you can do. But when I ordered it, I was told that both names had to be seven letters or less. My first name fit, but S's was one letter too long, so instead I had the rice writer use the first part of S's stage name—that is, the name under which he writes and posts his songs. That one's four letters long. In retrospect, I sort of wish I'd just had the rice writer call me "Barb" so that our names could be the same length. The only people who ever called me "Barb" were my parents, my sister, and my half brother—and, recently, one of my students, who goes by Zac, and who also goes by they, but is not Zachary Schoenhut. I'm not sure why Zac took to call-

fig 6.2 Rice Imre (B. Browning)

fig 6.3 Rice Barbara (B. Browning)

ing me Barb, but I like it. I hated being called Barb as a child, so I'm not sure why I like it when Zac calls me that. Anyway, all this made me wonder about calling S "*S*" in this writing, which is just one letter. And I wondered if it's because I'm calling myself "*I*."

lead paint and other poisons

....

In her lifetime, Sarah Biffen achieved some renown for her portrait miniatures, but she's not generally regarded as part of the art historical canon. That list usually begins with European manuscript illuminators. Illuminated manuscripts, technically, are decorated with either gold or silver marginalia (hence their luminescence), but the term *portrait miniature* comes, etymologically, from *minium,* a red pigment that is a naturally occurring form of lead tetroxide. This was the pigment often used by the early illustrators for their little likenesses of people, and in fact, it's the etymology of the word *miniature* in all its senses, though it's likely that the use of the term beyond the realm of painting had to do with its near homonymy with other words indicating smallness (*minor, minimus*) derived from the Proto-Indo-European *mei.* But back to the canon, which is a homonym of cannon, which is something we associate more with lead than art—though big cannonballs were rarely made of it. Most histories of the portrait miniature begin with Jean Fouquet and his six-centimeter-diameter self-portrait, circa 1450. This is

fig 7.1
Self-Portrait (J. Fouquet)
(Louvre)

also held to be the first signed self-portrait of any kind or size. I find it interesting that the first signed self-portrait in European art history is tiny.

The earliest painters of portrait miniatures were French and Flemish. Of the former, the most famous is Jean Clouet, who may have been the first to take the form out of the manuscript and onto discrete little rounds of vellum. Of the latter, the earliest renowned artist was Simon Bening, and his daughter Levina Teerlinc followed in his miniature footsteps. She took the practice to England, where she became a court artist under Henry VIII, Edward VI, Mary I, and Elizabeth I. The first native English portrait miniaturist of much renown was Nicholas Hilliard (1537–1619), followed by Samuel Cooper (1609–72), uncle of the poet Alexander Pope.

Actually, and perhaps not surprisingly, there are quite a few women artists who have been prominent in the genre. The Venetian Rosalba Carriera (1673–1757) began her career as a lacemaker, a skill she learned from her mother. When the market for lace started to falter, she got in on the snuff-box boom and started painting on the insides of the box lids to help out with the family expenses. She's reputedly the first person to paint miniatures on ivory. That worked out pretty well, and she moved to Paris. She got so many orders that she had her mother and her two sisters, Angela and Giovanna, working with her in her studio. Carriera became one of the most popular artists of her time. French and Italian poets eulogized her. But in 1738, Luisa Bergalli dedicated a collection of sonnets to Carriera's mother for having encouraged her daughters not to stick to lacemaking. She asked, rhetorically, "if heaven condemns us women / To working just with needle and with thread" (cited in "Rosalba Carriera"). Clearly not. Carriera didn't just paint miniatures—she also worked in pastels, which were another lightweight form and easy to transport. Her big stylistic innovation in pastels was to blur the sitter's image—a kind of early Photoshop solution for minor beauty flaws. Still, Carriera's self-portraits were notably not self-flattering. Art historians describe her as "resolutely single." When somebody proposed to her, she wrote back thanks but no thanks: "I have a cold, withdrawing nature" ("Rosalba Carriera"). But she supported younger female artists, and she really loved her sister Giovanna. When the sister died, Rosalba was disconsolate.

Among the first portrait miniaturists in the United States was Mary Roberts—maybe the first. She was born in England; we don't know when, but we know she died in Charleston, South Carolina, in 1761. The main source for any biographical information about her is the *South Carolina Gazette,* in which her husband took out a couple of ads offering his services as a painter—whether of portraits or houses. He also said he had a printing press. When he died in 1740, Mary took out her own ad, offering to paint portraits and also to sell the printing press. She was still trying to sell it in 1746. A couple of people left her and her apparently disabled son a little money, clothes, and furniture in their wills. She never signed her miniatures with her full name—just "MR," which of course looks like "mister."

*   *   *

You'll remember that my mother taught me to tat. Tatting is another word for lacemaking. My mother didn't limit herself to needle and thread. She was an art major in college. She never had ambitions to be a painter, but she was very good at drawing. When I was a child, she tried to teach me how to draw a face. She made an oval, with a line down the center, and another line, horizontal, at the midpoint. This, she said, was where the eyes should go. Halfway between that line and the chin, she drew another horizontal line, which was where the tip of the nose went, and again halfway between that line and the chin was where the mouth went. Try as I might, even with these guidelines, I never got good at drawing, and she didn't push it.

After the piano shop closed and my son had a lot of time on his hands, he decided he should learn how to draw. As a child, he, like me, showed no natural gift for draftsmanship. He texted me photos of a couple of his first efforts. The eyes were all too big and too high on the face, and the noses were tiny, which I think is fairly typical of self-taught portraitists. I asked him if he was consulting some kind of vade mecum to learn how to draw, and he said he'd watched a few YouTube videos. I liked his drawings—even this distinctly unflattering portrait of S and me in which I appear somewhat microcephalic. S's nose is also markedly diminished in size.

Leo didn't draw this from life, of course, but from a photograph he'd taken. He's an excellent photographer, although I confess that even the photo version of this portrait feels unflattering to me. That's because, unlike Rosalba Carriera, Leo doesn't generally blur out the beauty flaws. He likes very high contrast.

S has painted since childhood. There's a gouache on the wall here in New York that he did when he was about seven—a red sun exploding into a mustard yellow sky. He showed it to

fig 7.2
Drawing (L. Oliveira)

me in Normandy, and I asked him if we could bring it here. But as an adult, nearly all of his paintings have been on a tiny scale. Sometimes the format is large, but the figures are minuscule. We have another on the wall here, depicting a man in Arab dress crossing a desert, gazing down. He's passing two penguins. In the background, an old-fashioned horse-drawn carriage skirts the edge of a green sea, and further back still, two clouds float in an azure sky. You'd say it was a dreamscape, though it's made up of elements of real memories (S has spent time in the desert, in the Arctic, and by the sea). But he couldn't have remembered the green of the sea: he's red-green color blind.

S's style might also be called "naïf," but it's very scrupulous. He told me that in order to render the tiny details on his figures, he'll often pull out nearly every hair of a brush. Like me, over the years, he's come to rely on reading glasses, but that's the only magnification he uses, and he used to paint without any magnification at all. He finds this kind of painstaking process very calming. The paintbrushes used by the early miniaturists weren't, in fact, made with fewer hairs. They were full-bodied but came to a fine point. They were called "pencils." *Pencil* comes, etymologically, from the Latin word for tail. So does *penis*. So does *penicillin*.

* * *

Portrait miniatures are also called *limnings*. *Limn* is a homonym of *limb*. *Limn* comes from the Old French *luminer*, to light up. *Limb* comes from the Proto-Germanic *limu*, a small branch of a tree. Of course, the term *limning* has to do with portrait miniatures' origin in the illuminated manuscripts.

When Clouet took them out of books, they began to serve a different purpose: they could be carried around on one's person. Art historians often observe that looking at a portrait miniature is a very personal affair: you place yourself in the role of the intimate holder of a private image—much as the curators of that Frances Glessner Lee exhibit said that looking at her dioramas required you to get up close and personal with the scene of the crime. It's not unlike reading someone's personal correspondence. These portraits weren't intended for public display—they were intended for a particular viewer. This also has to do with the prominence of women in the form, just as women are among the most noted of epistolary writers. Well, I should perhaps also acknowledge that portrait miniatures, while ostensibly private objects, were also markers of class. Someone carrying one maybe didn't want people to get too close a look at it, but they might want people to notice that they had one. They were commodity fetishes with a high degree of sentimental value.

When European settlers came to the United States, they sometimes brought with them the little portable portraits of friends and family members they had left behind, just as the later German immigrants brought with them their little, portable toy pianos. Then people began commissioning portrait miniatures here. In *Love and Loss: American Portrait and Mourning Miniatures*, Robin Jaffee Frank considers the social changes that were taking place as the form developed in the United States—specifically, "an expanded market economy and a significant shift in social attitudes toward love, marriage, and family" (3). If you hold those things side by side, you may be unsettled because the notion of "companionate marriage," while appearing to counter the older model of unions based on strategic family alliances and units of labor, developed alongside (and arguably as a result of) market changes that depended on mercantilism and chattel slavery. And of course, legally, that's what marriage still was: a matter of property (though I should note that it was precisely in this period, and perhaps for the same reasons, that in the colonies white women were beginning to garner limited property rights). Market expansion was made possible by the exploitations of colonialism and the slave trade. Sentimental expressions, such as carrying a locket with a portrait of one's spouse, were the flipside of this coin—or of this locket.

Locket originally meant "the iron cross-bar of a window," from the Old French *loquet*, "a door-handle, bolt, latch, fastening," diminutive of *loc*, "lock, latch." There's a sequence of photos in Frank's book that shows the disassembled pieces making up a locket that held a portrait miniature of Benjamin Frederick Augustus Dashiell by the painter Robert Field. The pieces include the portrait, painted on an ivory wafer; a paper card "with goldbeater's skin still visible on the edges"; a convex glass oval framed with gold-plated copper; a cobalt-glass surround for the back, set into the gold-over-copper bezel with a hanger and ball finial attached; another protective convex glass with "teeth" in the bezel to hold it in the cobalt-glass surround; some crinkled metal foil covered with a magenta coating that, "when placed behind the cobalt glass, created a radiant effect"; a tiny lock of hair held together with gold wire and half pearls, mounted on opalescent glass; another piece of that magenta crinkled foil; and a little wad of folded newspaper for padding, to keep everything "snug" in there (8–9).

Each of these pieces is beautifully presented in the color photographs, though a couple of the pictures show the manipulations of the locket assembler: that battered card with the "goldbeater's skin still visible on the edges" and that wad of old newspaper. I tried to read the newsprint. All I could make out was: "prove/chamb/but the/the/fin//ed from the/the Secr/the/daries/ommitted/essage as."

The word *lock*, when referring to a bolt or door fastener, comes, like *locket*, from *loc*, but when it refers to hair, it comes from the Old English *locc*, from Proto-Germanic *lukkoz*, which may possibly come from Proto-Indo-European *lugnos*, related to the Greek *lygos*, "a pliant twig." The word *reluctance* is etymologically related—it's what happens when one doesn't feel so pliant.

A lock of hair is a fetish, however you want to look at it. At some point, a few years ago, S and I revealed to each other that we had little stashes of our own baby hair tucked away. He gave me some of his. I twined our locks together and put them in a locket and gave it to S. S had golden curls as a toddler, then long brown hair as a teenager, and then in his twenties his hair started falling out. I love his bald pate—more skin to kiss—but when he sees photos of his adolescent self, he sighs, staring at those cascading chestnut waves. People used to sometimes call him *mademoiselle*, but he defiantly kept his hair long until he started to lose it. I was born with a big shock of black hair, but that all fell out and grew back in, like S's, a golden brown, getting darker over time. Now of course there are a few white strands in the mix. But in the locket, it's hard to tell whose hair is whose.

Benjamin Frederick Augustus Dashiell had brown, wispy hair. You can see that in his portrait, but it was also incorporated into that locket, bound, as I said, with gold wire and half pearls. That is, I think it's Dashiell's hair in there, but some of it may have belonged to his wife. The lock is so artfully arranged, it doesn't look particularly human. Dashiell's portrait, I must say, is not particularly affecting to me. He looks a little smug. But maybe his wife or whoever carried that locket around found his slight smirk kind of adorable. Of all the pieces making up the locket, I'm most compelled by the little wad of enigmatic newsprint.

* * *

I've been fielding all kinds of paperwork and investigatory tasks related to the purchase of the house in the country. I found a lawyer and he advised me to have the inspector check for various possible poisonous things: radon, impurities in the water, any buried and possibly leaking old oil tanks, and lead paint. Fortunately, all of those checked out okay, although the inspector did say that a part of the house was constructed improperly, with the wood in direct contact with the soil, not on a concrete foundation. That held things up for a bit, as we had to have somebody else figure out how much it would cost to make it more secure. Because of COVID-19, the scheduling of things was even more complicated than usual. S was pretty blasé about the foundation question, since the previous owners had been living there for thirty years with no apparent problems. But I wanted to make sure it would be safe for another thirty. The house was built in 1953, when S was one year old. S is also generally pretty blasé about his own longevity. I'm the one who insists that he do a little yoga every morning and eat some fruits and vegetables.

When we first met, he said it made him a little sad that we met relatively late in our lives, partly because he thought our younger selves would have enjoyed each other, partly because it meant we might not have many years together. That was when we were fifty-three and sixty-two. I told him not to worry: by my calculation, we had plenty of time. I wrote him a lullaby called "We Have Twenty-Nine Years." That was, of course, a rough estimate. I still say that, and he says, "You made that estimate a while ago," but I answer, "That was before you quit smoking!" I figure that extended things. He doesn't really buy it, but it makes him smile. I also made the estimate before S's diagnosis of emphysema, or the global pandemic, but I maintain my perhaps Pollyannaish optimism, or realism, depending on your perspective.

The red paint in the bedroom in New York is not lead paint. I know, because Leo painted it about ten years ago.

* * *

The cover of Robin Jaffee Frank's book shows *Harriet Mackie (The Dead Bride)*, a portrait miniature painted by P. R. Vallée in 1804.

It's an unusual portrait, as it depicts the subject with her eyes closed. But it's representative of the increased use of miniatures for mourning from the eighteenth to the early nineteenth centuries. Frank says, "The growth of increasingly private, child-centered families made loss harder to bear and contributed to the miniature's popularity as a token of mourn-

fig 7.3
Harriet Mackie (P. R. Vallée)
(Yale Art Gallery)

ing" (7). That's one way of looking at it. Many mourning miniatures were made after larger portraits that were painted while the subject was still alive, but some were modeled on the corpse. Even these, however, usually represented the subject with the eyes open, as in life. Frank surmises that Vallée may have, "as was customary [in painting from corpses], ... secured Harriet's slack jaw with a strap and continued to work as decomposition set in" (141).

The portrait, of course, doesn't include a jaw strap, or any sign of rot, but there's a diary entry by a family acquaintance, John Blake White, that does:

> June 5th 1804. After but a few short hours illness death has snatched from our sight one to whom youth and health had promised length of days. But last evening I was at the house and in the society of Miss Harriott Mackey, and today I have beheld her a corpse! Merciful God! Is it possible, that a few hours shall have effected so great a change, as that the object which but yesterday seemed so lovely and so fair to view, should today appear disgusting and become the object of our aversion. (cited in Frank, 148)

That's pretty honest.

Frank says that Harriet Mackie's unexpected death was attributed, by some, to unnatural causes:

> Harriet's apparent "perfect health" and the unexplained rapidity of its decline created a mysterious local legend that she was poisoned. Although no clear evidence of foul play exists, a motive for murder can be found in the will left by Harriet's father, Dr. James Mackie, who died when she was seven. He

gave to his wife "a certain number of negroes, some cattle and horses and Fifty Pounds to buy a riding chair," and, as long as she remained his widow, "liberty to plant my land with her negroes under the direction of my Executors." Most important, his will made his daughter that rare phenomenon in early nineteenth-century Charleston society, a rich woman in her *own* right:

> I will and devise all the rest and residue of my Estate both real and personal consisting of negroes, horses, cattle, &c., to my daughter, Harriet Mackie when she attains the age of 21 years or at the day of her marriage which ever shall happen first. But if my said daughter should die before the above mentioned periods, then I give that part of my Estate which I have given to my said daughter, to Captain Wm. Alston's two sons, John Alston and Wm. Alston. (150)

The implication is, of course, that one or both of these Alston boys—the sons of "King Billy" Alston, possibly the largest slaveowner in South Carolina—might have had an interest in knocking Harriet off just before her wedding. Harriet's mother actually took King Billy to court for the estate, to no avail, but she didn't outright accuse anybody of poisoning her daughter.

It's tempting to read John Blake White's journal entry the same way that Swift's apologists read his references to the "filth" and "stink" of women generally—that is, as referring to what was really "disgusting": the slave system that made her family's wealth possible. That's also what made her portrait miniature possible. All this is true, but Harriet Mackie's corpse also stank, however delicate she appears in that locket. What's the poison in that paint?

* * *

The name of the private road where our future house sits is Clearwater Lane. S finds this name enchanting. It's funny, though, because the water surrounding the property is anything but clear: it's marshland, much of it covered in pea green murk. While marshlands may look murky, they're in fact important for filtering toxins out of water. More than half of the wetlands of the United States were lost to development since the mid-eighteenth century. Our future property abuts the Great Vly, a "wildlife management area." "Managing" the flora and fauna seems to mean two things: encouraging limited, sustainable fishing, trapping, and hunting, and discouraging development that would endanger the ecosystem.

"Vly" comes from the Dutch for swamp. In Afrikaans, a *vlei* is a shallow lake. In New York, like in South Africa, there are many place-names that come from the Dutch. Brooklyn was named after Breukelen, a Dutch town that meant either "broken land" (from the Dutch *breuk*) or "marshland" (from *broek*). The Bronx was named after Jonas Bronck, who immigrated to Nieuw Nederland in 1639 (he may have been born in Sweden or Denmark, and he may have emigrated due to religious persecution—unclear). Harlem comes from Haarlem, a once robust trading port outside Amsterdam. Nieuw Nederland began as a trading post of the West-Indische Compagnie. The WIC reported purchasing the island of Manhattan for trade goods valuing sixty guilders, or twenty-four dollars, paid to the Lenape people. According to the Lenape, however, who didn't believe in private ownership of land, the "payment" was a gift expressing appreciation for permission to share use of the land, which the Dutch claimed, exclusively, as property. The development of Nieuw Nederland was accomplished through the labor of African slaves, who began arriving in 1626. There were eleven of them in the first shipment. They were also ostensibly the "property" of the WIC.

New York City was also swampy. Fresh Water Pond was a body of fresh water in what's now Chinatown. It was the main source of water for the first two hundred years of European settlement on the island of Manhattan. Like the Great Vly, lower Manhattan was marshy. As the land surrounding Fresh Water Pond was developed, the pond became polluted and started to stink. There were lots of mosquitos. A badly engineered landfill was completed in 1811. The buildings constructed there had faulty foundations and poor drainage. Most of the middle- and upper-class residents fled, leaving the area to poor immigrants who began arriving in the 1820s. In 1838, the city constructed a jail on the site of the former pond. It was called "the Tombs." It was leaky and damp, and eventually it was condemned and demolished. In 1941, they built a new House of Detention across the street. It's still popularly referred to as the Tombs.

Fresh Water Pond, like Clearwater Lane, is a beautiful name. The lawyer just sent me paperwork on our future house. When I went through the title report, I noticed that the first documented owner appears to have been named Helen Emma Clearwater, who granted the deed to Joanne Anderson, who subsequently granted it, upon the payment of one dollar, to Pearl Clearwater. So evidently Clearwater Lane doesn't refer to the clarity of the water surrounding it. Pearl Clearwater is an especially beautiful name. And I find it interesting that the property was passed from woman to woman, in apparently nominal deals that sound more like gifts. But, of course, the water around the house is still murky.

* * *

The portrait miniature that astonishes me most was painted by Sarah Goodridge in 1828: *Beauty Revealed*. It's 2.6 inches by 3.1 inches, and it's housed in a tiny wooden box.

Goodridge painted it for Daniel Webster, the famous statesman, who was in all likelihood (hello) her lover. She was forty years old when she made it. Goodridge met Webster when he sat for her in 1825 (over the years, she made at least a dozen miniatures of him). When they first met, Webster was married, with three children, but they began a correspondence (she saved his letters, but he destroyed hers). When his wife died in 1828, Goodridge went to visit him, and I guess that's when she gave him this self-portrait, but he ended up marrying somebody else. When he separated from his second wife, in 1841, Goodridge visited again. He quietly held on to *Beauty Revealed* until he died, and it was found among his personal effects.

Goodridge never married. Some art historians have hinted that she may have given Webster this painting in hopes of getting a marriage proposal, but I'd prefer to think that she, like Carriera, was resolutely single. This version of the story is just

fig 7.4 *Beauty Revealed* (S. Goodridge)
(Metropolitan Museum of Art)

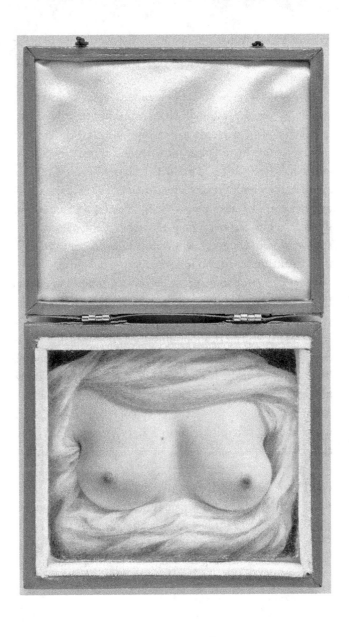

as suspect as any other, but not more. She did manage to make enough money on her own to support herself, an orphaned niece, and her elderly mother.

Perhaps you know something about Daniel Webster. He wasn't, to my eyes, especially handsome, but he's always remembered as an extraordinary orator—some say the greatest in our nation's history. His most famous speech was three-and-a-half hours long. It was delivered on March 7, 1850. It seems to me weird that this is remembered as a triumph of oratory, not just because it was so long, but also because it was, by all accounts, tactical and insidiously moderate. It was a response to John Calhoun, who'd urged the Senate to respect the institutions of the South—including, of course, slavery. Webster's response strategically defended a compromise solution, arguing against the institution of slavery in the new territories of the Southwest but tolerating the practice as it held in the South. Northern abolitionists were outraged, but moderates and businessmen found this great, and the only way of holding together the Union without war. Well, we all know how that went. How compelling could a speech like that be? Actually, I read the whole thing, and needless to say, it was horrifying. His ostensible view on slavery is that it's been done all over the globe, from time immemorial, and he claims that the way it evolved in the South was often with "care and kindness." More generally, his view of the United States is this: "In all its history, it has been beneficent; it has trodden down no man's liberty; it has crushed no state. Its daily respiration is liberty and patriotism; its yet youthful veins are full of enterprise, courage, and honorable love of glory and renown" (Webster).

I guess that made some people feel pretty good about themselves, even though it was a massive crock of shit.

I'm writing this in the fall of 2020. I'm very worried about the election in November and what will come after. I probably don't need to mention that.

Webster delivered that famous speech nine years after the dissolution of his second marriage. I wonder what his estranged wife thought about that. I also wonder what Sarah Goodridge thought. As I mentioned, he destroyed all her letters. He only kept her breasts. In 1850, Goodridge was starting to go blind. That's when she stopped painting.

It's hard to resist the temptation to say that *Beauty Revealed* is a selfie—or more specifically, a sext. It would fit very nicely on an iPhone. A few years ago, Karen Finley made a series of small portraits at the New Museum in New York. The project was called *Sext Me if You Can*. I wrote about it in a novel, but as in pretty much all my fiction, what I wrote really happened. This was the museum's description of the event:

> For this performance, Karen Finley creates a limited edition of paintings inspired by "sexts" that she receives from participating patrons. Participation takes the form of a commission and requires a ten-minute private and anonymous sitting on-site during announced performance times (bring your own cell phone!). Through this process, the erotic exchange with the artist—bound by rules of commerce—transforms into a lasting and collectible work of art. (New Museum)

Basically, you arranged the commission online ($200 for a small work on paper), and then you anonymously arrived at a

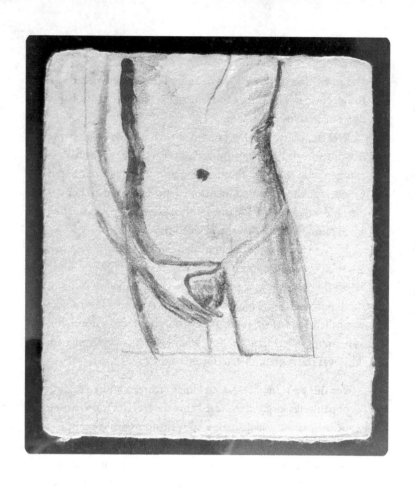

fig 7.5
Drawing (K. Finley)

storage room in the basement of the museum and texted Finley either a photo or a text, which she used to make her tiny portraits. Here's mine.

As you can see, I'd stripped and photographed myself touching my own sex. I know Karen, but I didn't tell her it was me. Like Sarah Goodridge, and like all cautious sexters, I didn't include my face. I sent Karen a few shots, a couple of which made my tattoo visible, so she could have recognized me, but she didn't. Sarah Goodridge's selfie shows the mole on her right breast, so she also could have been discovered.

Over the time we've known each other, I've sent S—especially during the periods of our separations—many portrait miniatures of myself. He keeps them safe on an external hard drive. They're among his personal effects.

I'm fifty-eight. I made that photo for Finley when I was fifty-one. Art historians seem surprised that Sarah Goodridge was forty when she gave Webster *Beauty Revealed*. Chris Packard suggests that the image is somewhat idealized and that Goodridge "costumed these breasts with youth, balance, paleness, and buoyancy." But I think it may have been an entirely realistic rendering. Forty's not so old, and Goodridge never had a baby. I nursed Leo for nearly three years, but on account of their diminutive size, my breasts remain pretty buoyant, if a little the worse for wear (there's a small dent on the right one from a lumpectomy—benign).

My mother lost one breast to cancer when she was in her forties. She was thirty-four when I was born, and she breastfed me. At the end of her life, when I'd help her dress and undress, I was surprised by how beautiful her remaining breast was. She thought so too. Younger, she'd been like me, very small-breasted, but after she lost one, the other plumped up, as if to compensate. In her eighties, her breast looked sort of like Sarah Goodridge's—actually, much more like that than the sunken dugs of that stuffed doll she made. So never mind what I said about her being a realist. I think Sarah Goodridge was probably a realist.

* * *

Last night, S told me the story of Agnès Sorel, the official mistress of Charles VII, who appeared in all her portraits with a single breast exposed. The most famous is by Jean Fouquet, the first miniaturist, though it's not a portrait miniature.

That one, obviously, is not so realistic. Sorel had a lot of influence over Charles VII. As S told me, she was one of three influential women in the king's life—the others being his wife and Joan of Arc. Agnès Sorel, like Harriet Mackie, died suddenly, possibly at the direction of Charles's son, who wasn't so happy about the sway she held over his father. A few years ago, forensic scientists unearthed Sorel's remains and tested them. They were full of mercury. She'd clearly been poisoned.

* * *

The portrait miniature began to decline as a genre with the advent of photography in the nineteenth century, but there was some overlap—literally, as some portrait miniaturists took to painting on the surface of daguerreotypes. The new technology is sometimes said to have "democratized" portraiture, putting it within the means of more people. It also seems to have encouraged more "ethnographic" portraiture—pictures identified not by an individual's name, but by their class, race, sex,

fig 7.6
Agnès Sorel (J. Fouquet)
(Royal Museum of Fine Arts, Antwerp)

or immigration status. And it evolved into new forms of self-portraiture, including the ones we now refer to as the selfie and the sext.

It wasn't long after the pandemic began that we began to see stories about how much sexting was going on, for obvious reasons. It didn't appear to be panicking too many people—in fact, there was a proliferation of articles and blog posts pointing out the ways in which sending little erotic self-portraits might help us to sustain each other in our isolation. Some of these came with the old caveats about cropping out your face and any identifiable markings, like tattoos, just in case your picture should fall into the wrong hands. Some came with other precautionary advice—like, given that we're all feeling somewhat vulnerable, this may not be the time to overdo it if the recipient isn't ready, and it may also not be the best time to "ghost" somebody if you're not feeling it yourself.

A self-portrait miniature can be a very sustaining gift. But the word *gift*, as I've pointed out before—and so have many others—is also German for "poison." And all portrait miniatures are a manner of "ghosting" people, whether we intend to or not.

that which is more
proportionable to the smallness
of my abilities

....

obert Hooke published *Micrographia: Or Some Physiological Descriptions of Minute Bodies Made by Magnifying Glasses with Observations and Inquiries Thereupon* in 1665. Despite the definition of *micrographia* that I gave you before—tiny handwriting— here, the term refers to the depiction and description of tiny things made possible by the developing technology of microscopy. Single-lens magnifying glasses were invented around the same time as corrective eyeglasses some four hundred years before, but compound microscopes first appeared in Europe in the early seventeenth century. Cornelis Drebbel, a Dutchman, is sometimes credited with making the first one. Another Dutchman, Antonie Philips van Leeuwenhoek, is often referred to as "the father of microbiology," but Hooke was the most important British figure in the early years of the field.

Hooke's book was the first popular account of microscopy, and he dedicated it, unsurprisingly, to Charles II. In the opening pages, he admits to the king that there are other scholars "now busie about *Nobler* matters: The *Improvement* of *Man-ufactures* and *Agriculture*, the *Increase* of *Commerce*, and the *Advantage* of *Navigation*.... Amidst all those *greater* Designs, I here presume to bring in that which is more *proportionable* to the *smallness* of my Abilities..." (ii–iii). But Hooke's book was a massive ham sandwich of observations and illustrations, some on fold-out plates that were four times the size of the folio.

"A ham sandwich of a book" is a metaphor, but in fact books serve as food for some creatures. You'll remember William Morton Wheeler's letter from the termite king. One of Hooke's enormous fold-out plates displays a drawing of "*the small Silver-colour'd* Book-worm." A bookworm is also a not-so-flattering metaphor for a certain kind of person. But Hooke waxes poetic on the real thing as he sees it under the microscope: it has, he says, "so many several shels, or shields that cover the whole body, every of these shells are again cover'd or tiled over with a multitude of thin transparent scales, which, from the multiplicity of their reflecting surfaces, make the whole Animal appear of a perfect Pearl-color" (208). He goes on about pearlescence and intricacy, and ends with an appreciative contemplation even of the bookworm's activities:

> indeed, when I consider what a heap of Saw-dust or chips this little creature (which is one of the teeth of Time) conveys into its intrals, I cannot chuse but remember and admire the excellent contrivance of Nature, in placing in Animals such a fire, as is continually nourished and supply'd by the materials convey'd into the stomach, and *fomented* by the bellows of the lungs; and in so contriving the most admirable fabrick

of Animals, as to make the very spending and wasting of that fire, to be instrumental to the procuring and collecting more materials to augment and cherish it self, which indeed seems to be the principal end of all the contrivances observable in bruit Animals. (210)

Hooke examines a few fabricated objects in *Micrographia,* including "*the Point of a sharp small Needle*," which, under the microscope, looks anything but sharp—blunt, "not round nor flat, but *irregular* and *uneven*" (2). Although he isn't explicit about it, the delirious descriptions and exquisite renderings of natural objects, juxtaposed with the ugly and awkward ones of human creations, have potential theological implications: humans are obviously not up to competing with the craftsmanship of, if you believe in such things, divinity. What's funny, though—or maybe this is the (blunt) point—is that some of the examples from nature are not the ones you'd expect to be singled out for their splendor.

The biggest plate in *Micrographia* is a gigantic engraving of a flea. "The strength and beauty of this small creature," Hooke says, "would deserve a description." The strength has to do with the clever articulations of its legs, which make it capable of all kinds of acrobatics. "But, as for the beauty of it, the *Microscope* manifests it to be all over adorn'd with a curiously polish'd suit of *sable* Armour, neatly jointed, and beset with multitudes of sharp pins, shap'd almost like Porcupine's Quills, or bright conical Steel-bodkins; the head is on either side beautify'd with a quick and round black eye" (210).

I can't say that Hooke's flea inspires in me quite that rapture, but I am moved by the detail of his etching, which I guess

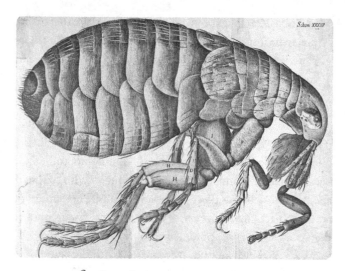

fig 8.1 *Flea* (*Micrographia*) (R. Hooke)

is sort of the opposite of what that implicit theological argument intended.

The year 1665 was not a good one for Londoners. In April, Margaret Porteous was the first (recorded) resident of the city to die of the plague. England and the Dutch Republic were battling over colonial possessions at the time, and it's been hypothesized that this outbreak of the plague on the British Isles was introduced by Dutch prisoners of war. In the next few weeks, two-thirds of the city residents fled London, but eventually, about a hundred thousand died—a quarter of the population. Next, the epidemic spread to Derbyshire. Meanwhile, in June, England installed a government in New York City, formerly known as New Amsterdam. On July 7, Charles II bailed, moving his court from London to Salisbury and later Exeter. In August, they decided to shut down the University of Cambridge, where Isaac Newton was studying. He bounced to Lincolnshire, where he holed up on his own for two years. Apparently, that wasn't such a bad decision, as he came up, in isolation, with various new theories he would later publish in *Philosophiæ Naturalis Principia Mathematica* and *Opticks*. It was in September that Robert Hooke published *Micrographia*, which became something like what we'd call a best seller. Obviously, you couldn't mail-order your books back then, so evidently some bookstores remained open, despite the raging epidemic. But things were pretty bleak. Here's an entry from Samuel Pepys's diary: "16 October 1665 But Lord, how empty the streets are, and melancholy, so many poor sick people in the streets, full of sores, and so many sad stories overheard as I walk, everybody talking of this dead, and that man sick, and so many in this place, and so many in that. And they tell me that in Westminster there is never a physitian, and but one apothecary left, all being dead—but that there are great hopes of a great decrease this week. God send it" (Pepys).

There's something Hooke doesn't mention in his rapturous description of the flea because nobody had figured it out yet: the flea was the vector of the plague. It was so tiny, and so consequential.

* * *

As you may have noticed, I'm a bookworm. That means that I have a robust appetite even for those tomes that most people think are past their shelf life. Maybe especially those ones. I'm not talking about the literary canon, of course, which gets revised all the time, because even those canonical works that fall out of favor feed the critiques. I'm talking about "secondary" literature: learned writings that end up dropping off syllabi and getting swept to obscure footnotes in academic journals and scholarly monographs, where all you're left with are the crumbs. You've already gotten a taste of some of that in this book. When I started researching microscopes, I found Marjorie Hope Nicolson. Now I can't get enough of her.

Nicolson was highly respected in her lifetime. She got her PhD at Yale in 1920 and taught at several universities before becoming the dean of Smith College in 1929. She later became the chair of the Department of English and Comparative Literature at Columbia. She was the first woman president of Phi Beta Kappa, the editor of *the American Scholar*, and, for a time, the president of the Modern Language Association. She wrote numerous books on the relationship between scientific discovery and literature in the seventeenth century—including *Science and the Imagination*, which contains her seminal essay, "The Microscope and English Imagination." In that work, and others, she demonstrated the ways in which scientific developments reconfigured what poets and writers were able to conceive of.

She was, with her teacher Arthur Lovejoy, an early proponent of the "history of ideas." All my graduate students now read Michel Foucault, who certainly taught us a lot about the "archaeology of knowledge," and sometimes you'll hear a reference to Lovejoy as a forebear, but it's largely the specialists who bother to cite Nicolson. Even on the relationship between scientific discoveries and literature in the seventeenth century, her work is mostly relegated to the references of scholars who foreground more explicitly colonial history and race politics (like Tita Chico) or sexuality and gender politics (like Raymond Stephanson and Deborah Armintor).

Chico reads a reference to Richard Ligon's *A True and Exact History of the Island of Barbadoes* in *Micrographia* as an implicit comparison of ants to slaves—demonstrating that what Hooke was looking at under the microscope was something very big and very politically charged, and he could see it only because of what he'd been reading. It's a tendentious interpretation, as all Hooke mentions in his description of the ant is "seemingly rational actions I have observ'd in this little Vermine with much pleasure, which would be too long to be here related; those that desire more of them may satisfie their curiosity in Ligons [*sic*] History of the *Barbadoes.*" Ligon's *History* does talk about the abuses of slavery, and it also talks about ants, without making explicit connections. I'm not sure if Hooke did make these connections, but reading Hooke reading Ligon certainly allowed Chico to see some very big things. I hope it will be clear that I have no aversion to tendentious and even exaggerated analyses based on scrupulous (one might say microscopic) close reading—something I sometimes attempt myself—nor to cross-species political analogies (particularly entomological ones, as you've seen). Marjorie Hope Nicolson tended to be a little more restrained in her interpretations.

Stephanson extends Nicolson's work to consider, quite graphically, seventeenth- and eighteenth-century preoccupations with male genitalia, and Armintor extends it to read the microscope as, effectively, a female phallus. Again, Nicolson showed greater restraint, or perhaps discretion.

"Miss Nicky," as she was known to her students, was by all accounts pretty intimidating. She thought all students of English literature needed to learn Latin, Greek, French, German, and Old English. She pronounced the word *class* "clahss." But she was very protective of her brood of doctoral advisees, if demanding—particularly of the women. She claimed never to have experienced discrimination in the profession, but she once observed, "the fundamental reason that women do not achieve so greatly in the professions as do men is that *women have no wives*" (cited in Thaddeus, 15). Despite not having a wife, she got a lot done.

* * *

A little over a year ago, S bought me a microscope as a gift. It wasn't in relation to this book I'm writing—he just thought I'd enjoy it. It was a gift he'd given all his children before, for the same reason. The technology has, of course, advanced over the years. The one he gave me is not especially strong in power, but it allows you to capture digital images of what you're looking at. We looked together at some predictable things—flower petals, grains of sugar and salt—and, most beautiful and remarkable, some molted skin of our pet lizard, Bölsche. Looking at it, we both made that perhaps banal observation that nature's artistry inevitably surpasses that of women and men.

It seems that couples poring over a microscope is something of a commonplace. Nicolson says that, in 1664, Samuel Pepys bought one and brought it home. His diary "noted the next evening that he and his wife had made their first observations 'with great pleasure, but with great difficulty before we could come to the manner of seeing anything by my microscope'"

(170). Nicolson also says that in 1710, Jonathan Swift bought a microscope for Stella. He wrote her just before purchasing it, with his typically weird forms of address, alternating between third and second person as well as feminine and masculine: "I doubt not it will cost me thirty shillings for a microscope, but not without Stella's permission; for I remember she is a *virtuoso*. Shall I buy it or no? 'Tis not the great bulky ones, nor the common little ones, to impale a louse (saving your presence) upon a needle's point; but of a more exact sort, and clearer to the sight, with all its equipage in a little trunk that you may carry in your pocket. Tell me, sirrah, shall I buy it or not for you?" (186).

Apparently, the answer was yes.

Nicolson thinks that microscopy influenced Swift in the writing of *Gulliver's Travels*, but this letter would indicate that in their household, the microscope was under Stella's dominion. Actually, that wasn't unusual. Nicolson writes that in the late seventeenth and early eighteenth centuries, women were increasingly attracted to new scientific technologies, particularly optical ones. When it came to the telescope and the microscope, Nicolson says, "of the two, the microscope naturally made the greater appeal to ladies. Easily obtainable at a not prohibitive price, it could readily be used by amateurs.... In a short time it became the ladies' toy" (185). (You can perhaps deduce from this Armintor's reasoning.) Advertisers marketed microscopes accordingly. They came with fancy, ornamental holders (bejeweled iPhone cases, of course, spring to mind). There was a name for the kind of young woman who went in for all that—actually, two. She was called either a "virtuosa" (see Swift, above, with his characteristic gender switcheroo) or "the scientific girl." Both of those terms were generally invoked with irony.

Mary Shelley and Octavia Butler were *virtuosas*. So is Donna Haraway. Paul Preciado was one, but now he's a *virtuoso*. Marjorie Hope Nicolson was also a *virtuosa*, though interestingly, she doesn't say that herself. I'm not a *virtuosa*, or at least I'm not a scientific girl. I gamely look over S's shoulder at the microscope, but, like my skills in drafting, my scientific observational capacities are pretty meager. I tend to stick to that which is more proportionable to the smallness of my abilities.

* * *

The writing of this chapter was interrupted for a period of about three weeks, as the mortgage finally came through, and my time was consumed by (on top of my online teaching schedule) legal and financial transactions, the setting in place of utilities and other services in the new house, and the transportation of some of our belongings. Because of our remote location, the only internet service available to us here is via satellite, which turns out to mean it's feeble and outlandishly expensive. We try to view this as an advantage (discouraging screen time), though at first it put me in something of a panic about my teaching. I managed to rig up something with my phone and a massive cellular booster attached to the roof, which improved things a little.

Unlike Miss Nicky, aside from my teaching, I haven't been getting a lot done. Little tasks seem very daunting, particularly when they involve communications. This has something to do with the lack of connectivity, digital or cellular—the lag for a file to up- or download is stultifying, and customer service lines, when I can reach them, invariably have a recording noting "longer-than-usual wait times" due to COVID-19. I know I'm not alone in these difficulties. Yet being not only a bookworm but also a type A person, I find it a little agonizing.

Once we got ourselves more or less installed, S and I began gardening, despite the lateness of the season, and that helped. We've also done some exploration through the Great Vly. S got a hold of a couple of those forehead-mounted flashlights that spelunkers use. Sometimes at night we creep into the woods, arm in arm, and stare back at the deer, whose eyes shine neon green. S gathered six frogs, one toad, and a couple of garter snakes, all of which he's placed in moss-lined terrariums. Throughout the day, between the frustrating attempts to get work done, we occasionally forage for insects to feed them and pause to watch the general pandemonium when we serve them up.

I miss my son.

A few other things happened since we arrived. One morning, I awoke to a text from Sarah announcing the death of David Graeber. That was a shock—to her as well as to me and a lot of other people. I'd met Graeber a couple of times, and in fact I'd written him into two of my novels (when I told him about the first one he seemed vaguely bemused, glancing at the back cover of the copy I'd just handed him with one eyebrow raised). I also emailed him another gift—a ukulele cover of Leo Ferré's "Les anarchistes" (to that, he sent a curt reply, pronouncing my version "pretty good"). That's not a lot of contact. But whenever I taught my course on theories of the fetish, I relied heavily on his own tendentious and perhaps exaggerated analysis of Marcel Mauss and gift economies, which

I found totally inspiring. Several others among my students wrote me when word got out, thinking I might have taken his passing hard, even though he wasn't what you could really call my friend. They were right. I took it hard. I cried intermittently for days.

When Sarah wrote me, I'd immediately wondered if Graeber's death was COVID-19 related, but it wasn't. Less baffling than this unexpected catastrophe, but no less surreal, was the sudden revelation of Donald Trump's contraction of the virus. I don't need to rehearse for you the whiplash of conflicting information regarding the gravity of his illness, and his loopy, manic statements, which appeared to be fueled by a steroid high—but then again, they were entirely consistent with plenty of his prior loopy, manic statements.

When you drive around here in the country, you pass some houses with Biden-Harris banners and rainbow and planet Earth flags. You also pass some with stars and stripes, and signs saying "TRUMP: NO BULLSHIT." There's a house down the road from us that doesn't say who they're voting for, but they encourage us to "Repeal the S.A.F.E. Act." That refers to New York State legislation passed in 2013 intending to prevent "criminals and the dangerously mentally ill from buying guns."

Mostly, we feel safer here than we did in New York City. Still, sometimes I'm afraid.

* * *

Robert Hooke is often credited with discovering and naming the cell, in the biological sense of that word. In *Micrographia*, he most famously describes vegetal matter (cork) as being made up of "walled" units like the solitary living quarters, or cells, of a monastery. That's Hooke's reputed association—the monastic one—but of course one could also make the link to cells of a prison. The word derives from the Latin *celare*, "to hide, conceal," and came into English usage in the twelfth century in reference to monks' quarters. The word wasn't extended to the notion of prison quarters, or other places of detention, until the eighteenth century.

Sometimes there's an overlap between these things. Foucault makes much of the brutal discipline at Bethlem Hospital (known as Bedlam), a London madhouse once housed in a monastery. But there's something he doesn't mention: in 1676, it moved to a new building, designed by Robert Hooke. Despite his modesty in the dedication of *Micrographia*, he wasn't only involved in tiny things.

I've been worrying about Karen Collins's son. I'm not sure where he is, but the California prison system is currently overwhelmed with COVID-19 cases. The last time I checked, at San Quentin, the rate of infection was 65 percent.

When we got here, we had more space. But, like everybody, we were also beginning to experience some fatigue. Under "normal" circumstances, I'm much more social than S, and it hasn't been easy for me to forgo collective pleasures. The online versions of these aren't without their charms, but even if you have a good internet connection, they hardly replace the exhilaration of a rousing graduate seminar, the mirth of a cocktail in a bar with friends, or the thrill (I know, I'm weird that way) of watching durational performance art in a dimly lit downtown experimental theater. S's sense of loss is of course much keener. There's a huge, uncrossable abyss between him and his house, his country, his language, and, most painful, his daughters—with no end in sight. He surely has more reason for despair than I—but we've both succumbed, on occasion, to moodiness. There have been a few moments of friction. I'm putting that mildly. The other day, he scrambled to escape my grouchiness, calling it "toxic," and I hurled the adjective right back at him. This, despite the ostensibly purifying capacities of the wetlands surrounding Clearwater Lane.

I find myself occasionally thinking of S not so much as my podmate, but my cellmate. I told you, the figure of speech is obscene under the circumstances, and I know it.

* * *

I texted Leo and asked him if we could meet on FaceTime. He told me he'd prefer to wait a week or two, as he didn't want to talk until he had something positive to report. He's been trying to sell a small piece of property his father left him. Given the restrictions in place due to COVID-19, this hasn't been easy. He probably won't end up with more than a few thousand dollars, but the first thing he wants to do is pay me back, as I fronted the cash for Tony's funeral. He thinks he should pay for that. I told you, this kind of thing runs in the family.

* * *

Among Marjorie Hope Nicolson's other publications on the relationship between literature and the history of knowledge is a book with the heart-rending title *"This Long Disease, My Life": Alexander Pope and the Sciences.* The study largely focuses on early eighteenth-century medicine, as Pope's various ailments made him something of a guinea pig among the physicians of his time. This, Nicolson posits, inflected his writing, sometimes in not so obvious ways. She opens the book with a "medical case history" of Pope's diverse maladies, which included dwarfism and severe curvature of the spine. In all likelihood, his kyphoscoliosis derived from a childhood case of tuberculosis of the bone, caused by his drinking unpasteurized milk. The *Oxford English Dictionary*, Nicolson tells us, defines kyphoscoliosis as a double, "backward and lateral curvature of the spine" (15). From the back, that is, the spine resembles the letter S, while from the side it resembles a question mark. Pope also had some gastroenterological and urinary difficulties, the latter possibly of gonorrheal origins. Nicolson cites some excruciatingly understated passages from his personal correspondence that make it clear he was in constant pain, though this is rarely explicit in his public writings.

Pope was about four foot six. He only fleetingly mentions his stature in *An Epistle to Dr. Arbuthnot* ("I cough like Horace, and tho' lean, am short"), but he did publish two brief articles in the *Guardian* about "The Club of Little Men," in which he claimed that "a Sett of us have formed a Society, who are sworn to *Dare to be Short*, and boldly bear out the Dignity of Littleness under the Noses of those Enormous Engrossers of Manhood, those Hyperbolic Monsters of the Species, the tall Fellows that overlook us" (cited in Nicolson, 10). Apparently, he sent out some invitations to people to join this club, but he didn't have a lot of takers. Still, his perspective as a little person may have marked at least one friend. "One wonders," Nicolson writes, "indeed, what details Swift might have picked up for his Lilliputians and Brobdingnagians from watching the actual experiences of his 'little friend'" (10).

Pope's correspondence also makes reference to his sense of smallness in a more figurative sense. He spent years tending dutifully to his sickly mother, despite his own infirmities. All that, combined, didn't make for a particularly active public life. In 1720, he wrote a friend, "I have not seen a play these twelve months, been at no assembly, opera, or public place whatever. I am infamously celebrated as an inoffensive unenvied writer" (27).

Whatever he or others might have made or might make of Pope's literary standing, physically, he was little, and as I mentioned earlier, he was the nephew of the famous miniaturist, Samuel Cooper. But the reason I wanted to think about him here—aside from the fact that I came to his biography through Marjorie Hope Nicolson—is that there's a striking and very weird scene in *This Long Disease, My Life* that deals explicitly with a microscope. In a later chapter titled "Pope and Other Sciences," Nicolson tells us that he, like many of his contemporaries, was indeed interested in the development of optics—both telescopes and microscopes—but due to vision problems (he had those too), it was "difficult if not impossible" for Pope to make use of those instruments himself. "It is significant," she writes, "that on the one occasion on which he referred to a real instrument it was his mother rather than Pope himself who made the observation." He wrote a letter to his friend John Caryll in 1718 recounting the visit of a clockmaker who was "likewise curious in microscopes and showed my mother some of the *semen masculinum*, with animascula in it" (248). Nobody—that is, neither Pope nor Nicolson—pauses to say that it's a little surprising that a visiting clockmaker showed a little old lady some semen under a microscope.

Animascula isn't really a word—Pope appears to have confused, or combined, Leeuwenhoek's term *animalcule*, a tiny living creature visible only under compound lenses, with *masculus*, male. In the seventeenth century, as you may know, it was popularly imagined that what we now call "spermatozoa" (that term only dates from the early nineteenth century) contained *homunculi*—miniature human beings that were deposited in the womb, where they would grow to baby size. Raymond Stephanson notes that while *homunculi* proliferated in the popular imagination, it was the "ovist school" that dominated scientific speculation at the time—that is, the notion that "the miniature human … reside[d] within the egg" (38).

That sounds a little bit like the story of Ms. Sphex and her spermatheca. I just realized that it's funny I called Nicolson's essay on microscopy "seminal."

* * *

We love the deer here in the country, but there is a downside: when we arrived, everybody began warning us about the prevalence of deer ticks and Lyme disease. Having lived so long near the forest in Normandy, S didn't take this very seriously. He's been intrepidly creeping through the Vly nearly every day, hunting for amphibians. But a couple of nights ago, he showed me a suspicious target-shaped red spot on his shoulder. We looked at each other. The next day, we arranged a glitchy teleconference with our doctor in New York who immediately prescribed him doxycycline hyclate. When I read up on this medication, I told him that another benefit was that it might prevent him from getting malaria. I was joking, of course. Actually, he's had malaria before. That's not really what we're worried about right now.

Naturally, this episode made me think of the shattering last lines of Wheeler's lecture "The Termitodoxa."

* * *

Perhaps you also know this: Alexander Pope and Jonathan Swift, along with their friends John Gay, John Arbuthnot, Henry St. John, Thomas Parnell, and Robert Harley, were members of the Scriblerus Club—a collection of satirists who took aim at scholarly pretention and the abuses of the "learned." They published, between 1713 and 1714, portions of the fictional *Memoirs of the Extraordinary Life, Works, and Discoveries of Martinus Scriblerus*, and some three decades later Pope put them out as a volume. Regarding the fictional hero's intellectual gifts, this about boils it down:

> How Martin become a grat Critick.
> IT was a most peculiar Talent in
> Martinus, to convert every Trifle
> into a serious thing, either in the way
> of Life, or in Learning. (73–74)

There's a partial list of his "Philosophical and Mathematical Works" at the end, of which I'll cite only the last: "The Number of the Inhabitants of London determin'd by the Reports of the Gold-finders, and the Tonnage of their Carriages; with allowance for the extraordinary quantity of the Ingesta and Egesta of the people of England, and a deduction of what is left under dead walls, and dry ditches" (160).

Obviously the Scriblerians were making fun of people like Martinus Scriblerus, but in truth, he's a pretty sympathetic character in the *Memoirs*—at least to me. In fact, much of the published volume treats not his pedantry (which, needless to say, I also find somewhat affecting), but his doomed, queer romance with Lindamira, for whom he falls at a freak show. He can't convince the authorities to sanctify their union, given that she shares a set of private parts with her conjoined twin, Indamora. After that fiasco, Martinus resorts to publishing his rambling and seemingly meaningless theses.

All this made me think of Zachary Schoenhut and their own affecting thesis on transcribbling and queer acts of archival disruption.

* * *

It seems to me a particularly cruel twist of fate that one of Pope's ailments was caused by an early bout of gonorrhea. Colley Cibber wrote a pretty nasty public letter in 1742 claiming that he'd had to pull the poet off a "diseased bawd" in a "house of carnal recreation" in his youth. Pope denied the charge, but one critic, Professor George Sherburn, says it's pretty clear that in his twenties, "Pope, conscious of his physical infirmity, put up a brave front at being a rake" (cited in Nicolson, 66).

I find Pope's face, at least in the existing portraits, extremely handsome. In fact, he looks a lot to me like S. If I were a bawd, and I suppose I am, though not, to my knowledge, diseased, I could definitely imagine the attraction. Coincidentally, S also has kyphoscoliosis, but a very, very minor case of it. He's of normal stature—perhaps a little on the small size by contemporary American standards, but probably right around the median height for a Frenchman of his generation. You wouldn't notice the curvature of his spine unless you looked for it. Sometimes it gives him a backache. Every morning, I make him get into child's pose on the rug, and I press hard along either side of his spinal column, working my way from the bottom to the top, encouraging it to straighten out. I have the illusion that over time, I'm making progress. I don't think he believes in this procedure, but I guess it feels good because he lets me try.

When my son was little, I sometimes used to ask him to walk on my back. I'd lie on my belly on the bed, and he'd lean his hands against the wall for balance and tread up and down on either side of my spine. He certainly couldn't do that today— not that he'd be willing if I asked. His feet are size thirteen. He'd squash me like a bug.

* * *

We drove to the local post office today. It's only open in the afternoons, and the guy who runs it lives upstairs in the little house where it's located. We have a PO box there, since, as I mentioned, the United States Postal Service doesn't deliver on our private road. The only thing in our PO box was the deed to our house, sent by the lawyer now that all the closure dust has settled. When I opened it, I read: "WITNESSETH, that the party of the first part [that is, the seller], in consideration of ONE dollars [*sic*] lawful money of the United States . . . does hereby grant and release unto the party of the second part [that is, me], their heirs or successors and assigns of the party of the second part forever, All that certain plot, piece or parcel of land, with the buildings and improvements thereon erected." So, it was evidently my naïveté that made me think that string of deeds transferred from Helen Emma Clearwater to Joanne Anderson to Pearl Clearwater represented some sort of utopian feminist gift economy. It seems deeds are always just a charade of nominal transactions, with the "real" terms laid out elsewhere.

At first, of course, I was sad to have my utopian bubble burst, and then I wondered if I shouldn't rather be grateful for this document, which makes our house look like somebody's gift of an amazing bargain. Well, the house was a gift, though not from the party of the first part. If you trace it way back, it was a theft from the moment it became a property, long before the arrival of the Helen Clearwater. If you take it from the moment I bought it, it was sort of a gift from my mother, despite her lifelong commitment to the idea of a self-made woman. We all know that the figure of the self-made man is a peculiar American fiction. When you try to explain it to anybody from anyplace else in the world, they glaze over in disbelief. About a decade ago, Elizabeth Warren gave a famous speech saying it was bullshit. In 2017, Arnold Schwarzenegger, of all people, gave a speech saying the same thing. Everybody took that as an implicit attack on Trump. But even Americans who know better sometimes cling to the idea of a specifically American capacity for self-creation.

In 1859, Frederick Douglass gave a lecture titled "Self-Made Men." He opened it conceding that, "Properly speaking, there are in the world no such men as self-made men." Still, he couldn't help extolling "the men who owe little or nothing to birth, relationship, friendly surroundings; to wealth inherited or to early approved means of education; who are what they are, without the aid of any of the favoring conditions by which other men usually rise in the world and achieve great results." Obviously, that would include himself. In 1893, Eugene Debs published an editorial about self-made men in *Locomotive Firemen's Magazine*. He, too, said the term was "seemingly paradoxical—since men who rise from obscurity to eminence in any of the walks of life, must have been assisted by agencies quite independent of themselves" (267) (there's no mention of the fact that some of those "agencies" are, hello Miss Nicky, *wives*). But he goes on to redeem the term in a kind of "pull yourself up by the bootstraps" rallying cry to resigned and unambitious low-level railroad workers. He tells them they should look to certain exemplary political figures for inspiration— like Abraham Lincoln and … Daniel Webster.

My father, who grew up on a subsistence farm and only got to college and then graduate school on account of the GI Bill, loved the song "God Bless the Child." I think he thought it was about him. He evidently didn't think the of the GI Bill benefits as a "gift." Maybe as a crust of bread and such. Billie Holiday says in her autobiography that she wrote that song after an argument over money with her mother. When Billie tried to hit her up for some cash, her mother answered, "God bless that child that's got his own" (101). Knowing that makes the song, I think, very sad. It's true that it never made me sad when my mother said that kind of thing, but then again, I was never desperate for a fix.

* * *

When Marjorie Hope Nicolson retired, they held a big celebratory dinner for her at Columbia, and four eminent poets, her colleagues, delivered a "Garland of Verses" for her. My favorite is that proffered by the least famous of them, John Unterecker, who remembered that for seventeen years, in a "neat, cramped hand," she'd scribbled editorial notes on his manuscripts. He'd often crumple up his failed attempts, only to retrieve them in order to look at one of her marginal comments ("'Honest,' say, or 'fair . . .'"), realizing that somewhere along the line, her reading of him had become "definitive, inevitable." She evidently told him once, "I have all I can do to keep up with the day's work."

> . . . and I, who let,
> Sometimes, the day's work slide, think: "More
> Valuable perhaps than knowledge or than wit
> Are the daily household virtues. Only from these,
> Shaped by the mind, can greatness rise."
> And then I hear, somewhere, you saying just that. . . .

I wonder if she really said just that. Her notes were "not marginalia, then," Unterecker concedes, "but text" (cited in Hoffman, 406). She liked to write in pencil, but she evidently left a mark.

She had one student named Rosalie Colie, who wrote a tribute to her teacher in 1965. Colie called her "an extraordinary woman: frightening, commanding, compelling, admirable, irrevocably lovable (if one dares to love), larger than life, for whom one must readjust the proportion of one's thoughts. Such people are never easy to live with, precisely because of their size: they remind us, willy-nilly, of our own scale" (470). Physically, Nicolson was also quite small, though at the end of her life, like my mother, a little plump.

As I said, Nicolson thinks that Pope didn't make much use of optical lenses himself, but prior to that visit from the clockmaker, he did show an interest in telescopic discoveries. In his twenties, he probably attended some of the coffeehouse lectures of William Whiston, an astronomer, and it seems that hearing about the telescopic perspective on the immensity of the heavens left him unsettled. He wrote a friend: "You can't wonder my thoughts are scarce consistent, when I tell you how they are distracted! Every hour of my life, my mind is strangely divided. This minute, perhaps, I am above the stars, with a thousand systems about me, looking forward into the vast abyss of eternity, and losing my whole comprehension in the boundless spaces of the extended Creation, in dialogues with Whiston and the astronomers; the next moment I am below all trifles, even groveling . . . in the center of nonsense" (137–38). Nicolson observes: "Like many before and after, Pope experienced a dual response to [the] vastness [made visible by telescopy]—an expansion of his imagination, countered by a poignant awareness of the insignificance of man in a universe that had grown too vast for his comprehension" (149).

S thinks we should invest in a telescope now that we have an unobstructed prospect on the sky. I think that if we get one, I may once again not make the best use of it. We already have some binoculars, and when S tries to get me to focus on some distant bird of prey, I always have trouble finding it, and then adjusting the lenses for a clear view. But even if I could take in all that distance, I don't think it would alter my sense of insignificance. That's something else.

I went back and reread the soliloquy at the end of *The Incredible Shrinking Man.* I really can't say that out there on the deck, under the night sky, feeling my body dwindling, melting, becoming nothing, my fears melted away, and in their place came—acceptance.... But I'm not sure that's what I want—though maybe that's silly to say because "acceptance" is all about *not* wanting. I still want something that's not not wanting.

* * *

In the last couple of weeks before we left New York, a lot of other people were abandoning the city, and we picked up a couple of items of furniture they'd left on the street. One was a tiny chair—evidently crafted as a little plant stand. It would serve nicely for a person of a height of about sixteen inches. S insisted on bringing it here, and that was okay with me. I placed it against one wall, discreetly positioned facing the normal-sized armchairs and couch. I don't think we'll put a plant on it. I prefer to leave it there, empty like that, waiting for someone the right size.

WORKS CITED OR
OBLIQUELY REFERENCED

....

AFRICAN AMERICAN MINIATURE MUSEUM. "African American Miniature Museum: A Journey through Black History in Miniature." Accessed July 26, 2021. https://www.africanamerican miniaturemuseum.com/.

ARMINTOR, DEBORAH NEEDLEMAN. "The Sexual Politics of Microscopy in Brobdingnag." *Studies in English Literature, 1500–1900* 47, no. 3 (2007): 619–40.

BERLANT, LAUREN, AND KATHLEEN STEWART. *The Hundreds.* Durham, NC: Duke University Press, 2019.

BERMUDEZ, ESMERALDA. "Shadow Boxes Shed Light on African American History." *Los Angeles Times*, August 7, 2011. https:// www.latimes.com/local/la-xpm-2011-aug-07-la-me-miniatures -20110807-story.html.

BÖLSCHE, WILHELM. *The Triumph of Life.* Translated by May Wood Simons. Chicago: C. H. Kerr, 1913.

BRETON, ANDRÉ. *Nadja.* Translated by Richard Howard. New York: Grove, 1960.

BROWN, LAURA. "Reading Race and Gender: Jonathan Swift." *Eighteenth-Century Studies* 23, no. 4 (1990): 425–43.

BRUNNERSUM, SOU-JIE. "Dutch PM Deems Black Pete Tradition Racist." *DW*, June 5, 2020. https://www.dw.com/en/dutch-pm -deems-black-pete-tradition-racist/a-53700075.

BUTLER, OCTAVIA. *Bloodchild and Other Stories*. New York: Seven Stories, 1995.

CANBY, VINCENT. "Lily Tomlin, Shrinking Woman." *New York Times*, January 30, 1981.

CARROLL, LEWIS. *Alice's Adventures in Wonderland*. 1865. Reprint, London: Puffin, 2015.

CARSON, RACHEL. *The Sea around Us*. Oxford: Oxford University Press, 1951.

CARSON, RACHEL. *Silent Spring*. Boston: Houghton Mifflin, 1962.

CHRISTIE'S. "Rosalba Carriera: The Pastellist Whose 'Images Came from Heaven.'" July 17, 2020. https://www.christies.com/features /the-life-and-art-of-venetian-artist-rosalba-carriera-10796-1.aspx.

COLIE, ROSALIE. "O Quam Te Memorem, Marjorie Hope Nicolson!" *American Scholar* 34, no. 3 (1965): 463–70.

COLUM, MARY M. "Jonathan Swift." *Saturday Review of Literature*, November 22, 1930, 357–58.

DARROCH, GORDON. "Rutte's Recognition of 'Systematic Problem' of Racism Is a Watershed Moment." DutchNews.nl, June 4, 2020. https://www.dutchnews.nl/news/2020/06/ruttes-recognition -of-systemic-problem-of-racism-is-a-watershed-moment/.

DAVIS, ANGELA Y. *Are Prisons Obsolete?* New York: Seven Stories, 2003.

DEBS, EUGENE. "Self-Made Men." *Locomotive Firemen's Magazine* 17, no. 4 (1893): 267–71.

DERRIDA, JACQUES. *La carte postale*. Paris: Flammarion, 1979.

DEVPOST. "Transcribble." Accessed July 26, 2021. https://devpost .com/software/transcribble.

DE WAAL, ANASTASIA. "Barbie in the Microwave." *Guardian*, December 22, 2005. https://www.theguardian.com/lifeandstyle /2005/dec/22/shopping.

DOSCHER, PHOEBE. "42nd Annual Croll Lecture: Scrutiny in the Eighteenth Century by Tita Chico." *Gettysburgian*, November 1, 2019. https://gettysburgian.com/2019/11/42nd-annual-croll-lecture-scrutiny-in-the-eighteenth-century-by-tita-chico/.

DOUGLASS, FREDERICK. "Self-Made Men (1872)." Accessed July 26, 2021. http://www.leeannhunter.com/english/wp-content/uploads/2015/01/Douglass_SelfMadeMan1872.pdf.

DUTCH ART INSTITUTE. "Home: Dutch Art Institute." Accessed July 26, 2021. https://dutchartinstitute.eu.

ENCYCLOPEDIA.COM. "Marjorie Hope Nicolson." Accessed July 26, 2021. https://www.encyclopedia.com/people/social-sciences-and-law/education-biographies/marjorie-hope-nicolson.

EVANS, MARY ALICE, AND HOWARD EVANS. *William Morton Wheeler, Biologist*. Cambridge: Harvard University Press, 1970.

FERENCZI, SÁNDOR. "Gulliver Phantasies." *International Journal of Psychoanalysis* 9 (1928): 283–300.

FERENCZI, SÁNDOR. *Thalassa: A Theory of Genitality*. 1924. Reprint, London: Routledge, 1989.

FOUCAULT, MICHEL. *Discipline and Punish*. Translated by Alan Sheridan. New York: Vintage, 1995.

FRANK, ROBIN JAFFEE. *Love and Loss: American Portrait and Mourning Miniatures*. New Haven, CT: Yale University Press, 2000.

FREUD, SIGMUND. "Fetishism." In *The Standard Edition of the Complete Psychological Works of Sigmund Freud*, translated by James Strachey, 21:147–57. London: Hogarth Press and the Institute of Psycho-Analysis, 1961.

FREUD, SIGMUND, AND CARL JUNG. *The Freud/Jung Letters: The Correspondence between Sigmund Freud and C. G. Jung*. Edited by William McGuire. Translated by Ralph Manheim and R. F. C. Hull. Cambridge, MA: Harvard University Press, 1974.

GAREN, MICAH, MARIE-HELENE CARLETON, AND JUSTINE

SWAAB. "Zwarte Piet: Black Pete Is 'Dutch Racism in Full Display.'" *Al Jazeera*, November 27, 2019. https://www.aljazeera.com/features/2019/11/27/zwarte-piet-black-pete-is-dutch-racism-in-full-display.

GILMAN, CLAIRE. "Foreword." *Dickinson/Walser: Pencil Sketches*. Accessed July 26, 2021. https://issuu.com/drawingcenter/docs/drawingpapers109_dickinsonwalser.

GIOANNI, HENRI, ANNIE SANSONETTI, AND MOHAMED BENNIS. "Characteristics of Cervico-Ocular Responses in the Chameleon." *Visual Neuroscience* 14, no. 6 (1997): 1175–84.

GOLDBERG, WHOOPI. *Alice*. New York: Bantam, 1992.

GRAEBER, DAVID. *Toward an Anthropological Theory of Value: The False Coin of Our Own Dreams*. New York: Palgrave Macmillan, 2001.

GREENACRE, PHYLLIS. "The Fetish and the Transitional Object." *Psychoanalytic Study of the Child* 24, no. 1 (1969): 144–64.

GREENACRE, PHYLLIS. *Swift and Carroll: A Psychoanalytic Study of Two Lives*. Madison, CT: International Universities Press, 1955.

GRIMM, JACOB, AND WILHELM GRIMM. *Snow White and Other Stories*. New York: G. W. Jacobs, 1922.

GRONBERG, TAG. *Vienna: City of Modernity, 1890–1914*. New York: Peter Lang, 2007.

GROSE, FRANCIS. *Classical Dictionary of the Vulgar Tongue*. London: S. Hooper, 1788.

HAMMOND, EUGENE. *Jonathan Swift: Irish Blow-In*. Newark: University of Delaware Press, 2016.

HAMMOND, EUGENE. *Jonathan Swift: Our Dean*. Newark: University of Delaware Press, 2016.

HARAWAY, DONNA J. *Primate Visions: Gender, Race, and Nature in the World of Modern Science*. New York: Routledge, 1989.

HARAWAY, DONNA J. *Simians, Cyborgs, and Women: The Reinvention of Nature*. New York: Routledge, 1991.

HOFFMAN, DANIEL G., LOUIS SIMPSON, JOHN UNTERECKER, AND MARK VAN DOREN. "A Garland of Verses for Marjorie Hope Nicolson." *American Scholar* 31, no. 3 (1962): 404–7.

HOLIDAY, BILLIE, AND WILLIAM DUFTY. *Lady Sings the Blues*. 1956. Reprint, New York: Crown, 2011.

HOOKE, ROBERT. *Micrographia: Or Some Physiological Descriptions of Minute Bodies Made by Magnifying Glasses with Observations and Inquiries Thereupon*. London: Royal Society, 1665.

HURWITZ-GOODMAN, JACOB. "A Journey through Black History in Miniature." Atlas Obscura. Accessed July 26, 2021. https://www.atlasobscura.com/videos/african-american-miniature-museum-history.

IMDB. "The Incredible Shrinking Man." IMDB. Accessed July 26, 2021. https://www.imdb.com/title/tt0050539/characters/nm0930695.

JARRELL, RANDALL. *The Animal Family*. New York: Harper and Row, 1965.

KROPOTKIN, PËTR A. *Mutual Aid: A Factor of Evolution*. London: Heinemann, 1904.

LEMEIGNAN, MADELEINE, ANNIE SANSONETTI, AND HENRI GIOANNI. "Spontaneous Saccades under Different Visual Conditions in the Pigeon." *Neuroreport* 3, no. 1 (1992): 17–20.

LEONARD, ELMORE. *LaBrava*. New York: Arbor House, 1983.

LERNER, BEN. "Robert Walser's Disappearing Acts." *New Yorker*, September 3, 2013. https://www.newyorker.com/books/page-turner/robert-walsers-disappearing-acts.

LIGON, RICHARD. *A True and Exact History of the Island of Barbadoes*. London: Humphrey Moseley, 1657.

MATHEWS, HARRY, AND ALASTAIR BROTCHIE, EDS. *Oulipo Compendium*. Los Angeles: Make Now Press, 2005.

MAUSS, MARCEL. *The Gift: Forms and Functions of Exchange in Archaic Societies*. Translated by W. D. Halls. New York: W. W. Norton, 2000.

MERRIAM-WEBSTER, s.v. "contact." Accessed July 26, 2021. https://
www.merriam-webster.com/dictionary/contact.

MEYER, KATHLEEN. *How to Shit in the Woods*. Berkeley, CA: Ten
Speed Press, 1994.

MONTAIGNE, MICHEL DE. "Of Experience." *The Complete Essays of
Michel de Montaigne*. Translated by Charles Cotton. Delhi: Lec-
tor House, 2019.

MORSE, ERIK. "The Little Man of Nuremberg: Wonder in the Age
of Matthias Buchinger." *Paris Review*, March 17, 2016. https://
www.theparisreview.org/blog/2016/03/17/the-little-man-of
-nuremberg/.

MY STRENGTH AND MY SONG (BLOG). "Handwriting Analysis of
Emily Dickinson." Accessed July 26, 2021. https://strengthandsong
.wordpress.com/2010/12/22/handwriting-analysis-of-emily
-dickinson/.

NEW MUSEUM. "'Sext Me If You Can' by Karen Finley: Performance
and Installation." Accessed July 26, 2021. https://www.new
museum.org/calendar/view/150/sext-me-if-you-can-by-karen
-finley-performance-and-installation.

NICOLSON, MARJORIE HOPE. *Science and Imagination*. Hamden,
CT: Archon, 1976.

NICOLSON, MARJORIE HOPE, AND G. S. ROUSSEAU. *"This Long
Disease, My Life": Alexander Pope and the Sciences*. Princeton, NJ:
Princeton University Press, 1968.

NIELSEN, NIKOLAJ. "Dutch PM Tells People to 'Act Normal, or Go
Away.'" *EUobserver*, January 24, 2017. https://euobserver.com
/political/136641.

PACKARD, CHRIS. "Self-Fashioning in Sarah Goodridge's Self-
Portraits." *Common-Place* 4, no. 1, (2003). Accessed July 26, 2021.
http://commonplace.online/article/self-fashioning-in-sarah
-goodridges-self-portraits/.

PEPYS, SAMUEL. *The Diary of Samuel Pepys*. New York: Modern Library, 2001.

PEPYS, SAMUEL. "Monday 16 October 1665." Accessed July 26, 2021. https://www.pepysdiary.com/diary/1665/10/16/.

PILKINGTON, LAETITIA. *Memoirs of Laetitia Pilkington*. Athens: University of Georgia Press, 1997.

POPE, ALEXANDER. "Epistle to Dr. Arbuthnot." Accessed July 26, 2021. https://www.poetryfoundation.org/poems/44895/epistle-to-dr-arbuthnot.

POPE, ALEXANDER. *Memoirs of the Extraordinary Life, Works, and Discoveries of Martinus Scriblerus*. London: George Faulkner, 1741.

PRECIADO, PAUL B. *Testo Junkie: Sex, Drugs, and Biopolitics in the Pharmacopornographic Era*. Translated by Bruce Benderson. New York: Feminist Press, 2013.

RAWSON, CLAUDE. "Some Modest Proposals." *Times Literary Supplement*, March 17, 2017. https://www.the-tls.co.uk/articles/swift-modest-proposals/.

RICHTER, SARAH. "'In the Shell of the Old': Shelter, Anarchy, Property, and Performance." PhD diss., NYU, forthcoming.

ROBERTS, CHADWICK. "'Lily White': Commodity Racism and the Construction of Female Domesticity in *The Incredible Shrinking Woman*." *Journal of Popular Culture* 43, no. 4 (2010): 801–2.

ROBINSON, ELAINE. *Gulliver as Slave Trader: Racism Reviled*. Jefferson, NC: McFarland, 2006.

SANDER, ECKHARD. *Schneewittchen: Märchen oder Wahrheit? ein lokaler Bezug zum Kellerwald*. Gudensberg: Wartberg Verlag, 1994.

SANSONETTI, ANNIE. "Stage Directions for Trans Girls in Love: Gloss." Accessed July 26, 2021. https://imaginedtheatres.com/stage-directions-for-trans-girls-in-love-gloss/.

SCHNORE, LEO F. "The Legacy of Tatum's Art." *Journal of Popular Culture* 2, no. 1 (1968): 99–105.

SCHOENHUT, A. *Forty Years of Toy Making, 1872–1912*. Philadelphia: A. Schoenhut, 1975.

SCHOENHUT, ZACHARY. "transcribbling: queer acts of archival disruption." Master's thesis, Dutch Art Institute.

SEBALD, W. G. "Le Promeneur Solitaire: W. G. Sebald on Robert Walser." *New Yorker*, February 6, 2014. https://www.newyorker .com/books/page-turner/le-promeneur-solitaire-w-g-sebald -on-robert-walser.

SHELLEY, MARY. *Frankenstein, or The Modern Prometheus*. New York: Penguin Classics, 2018.

SHEPPARD, NANCI, AND DONNA LESLIE. *Alitji in Dreamland*. Berkeley, CA: Ten Speed Press, 1992.

SHERBURN, GEORGE WILEY. *The Early Career of Alexander Pope*. Oxford: Clarendon Press, 1934.

SIDDIQUE, HAROON. "Charlie and the Chocolate Factory Hero 'Was Originally Black.'" *Guardian*, September 13, 2017. https:// www.theguardian.com/books/2017/sep/13/charlie-and-the -chocolate-factory-hero-originally-black-roald-dahl.

SIMPSON, PATRICIA ANN. "Albert Frederick Schoenhut." Accessed July 26, 2021. https://www.immigrantentrepreneurship.org /entries/albert-frederick-schoenhut/.

SINGH, JULIETTA. *No Archive Will Restore You*. Santa Barbara, CA: Punctum, 2018.

SINGH, JULIETTA. *Unthinking Mastery: Dehumanism and Decolonial Entanglements*. Durham, NC: Duke University Press, 2018.

SINGH, JULIETTA, AND BARBARA BROWNING. "No Archive Will Restore You: Julietta Singh and Barbara Browning." *Women and Performance: A Journal of Feminist Theory* 29, no. 3 (2018): 339–45.

SMITHSONIAN AMERICAN ART MUSEUM. "Murder Is Her Hobby:

Frances Glessner Lee and the Nutshell Studies of Unexplained Death." Accessed July 26, 2021. https://americanart.si.edu /exhibitions/nutshells.

STEPHANSON, RAYMOND. *The Yard of Wit: Male Creativity and Sexuality, 1650–1750*. Philadelphia: University of Pennsylvania Press, 2003.

STRATTON, JON. *Writing Sites: A Genealogy of the Postmodern World*. Ann Arbor: University of Michigan Press, 1990.

STUBBS, JOHN. *Jonathan Swift: The Reluctant Rebel*. New York: W. W. Norton, 2017.

SWIFT, JONATHAN. *Gulliver's Travels*. 1726. Reprint, Oxford: Oxford World's Classics, 2008.

TAYLOR, ERIN. *Alice's Wonderful Adventures in Africa*. Self-published, 2019.

TERRY, RICHARD. "Review of Gulliver as Slave Trader: Racism Reviled by Jonathan Swift by Eleanor L. Robinson." *Scriblerian and the Kit-Cats* 42, no. 1 (2009): 66–67.

THACKERAY, WILLIAM MAKEPEACE. *The English Humorists of the Eighteenth Century*. London: Grey Walls Press, 1949.

THADDEUS, JANICE. *When Women Look at Men*. New York: Harper, 1963.

THOMPSON, NELLIE L. "A Measure of Agreement: An Exploration of the Relationship of D. W. Winnicott and Phyllis Greenacre." *Psychoanalytic Quarterly* 77, no. 1 (2017): 251–81.

VINCENT-FUMET, ODETTE. *Pluck—chez les abeilles*. Montreal: Éditions Beauchemin, 1942.

VINCENT-FUMET, ODETTE. *Pluck—chez les fourmis*. Montreal: Éditions Beauchemin, 1942.

VINCENT-FUMET, ODETTE. *Pluck—ses aventures*. Montreal: Éditions Beauchemin, 1942.

WALSER, ROBERT. *The Assistant*. Translated by Susan Bernofsky. New York: New Directions, 2007.

WALSER, ROBERT. *Microscripts*. Translated by Susan Bernofsky. New York: New Directions, 2012.

WASMANN, ERICH. *Die hl. [heilige] Hildegard von Bingen als Natur-forscherin* [St. Hildegard of Bingen as Natural Scientist]. Munich: J. Kösel, 1914.

WEBSTER, DANIEL. "Seventh of March Speech." Accessed July 26, 2021. https://www.ushistory.org/documents/seventh_of_march.htm.

WEBTOON. "Transcribbles." Accessed July 26, 2021. https://www.webtoons.com/en/challenge/transcribbles-/list?title_no=340213&page=1.

WEISMANN, AUGUST. *Das Keimplasma: Eine Theorie der Vererbung*. Jena: Gustav Fischer, 1892.

WEST-EBERHARD, MARY JANE. "Howard E. Evans: Known and Little-Known Aspects of His Life on the Planet." *Journal of the Kansas Entomological Society* 77, no. 4 (2004): 296–322.

WHEELER, WILLIAM MORTON. *Foibles of Insects and Men*. New York: Knopf, 1928.

WHEELER, WILLIAM MORTON. *Social Life among the Insects*. New York: Harcourt, Brace, 1923.

WIKIPEDIA. "Graham Technique." Accessed July 26, 2021. https://en.wikipedia.org/wiki/Graham_technique.

WIKIPEDIA. "Laetitia Pilkington." Accessed July 26, 2021. https://en.wikipedia.org/wiki/Laetitia_Pilkington.

WIKIPEDIA. "Matthias Buchinger." Accessed July 26, 2021. https://en.wikipedia.org/wiki/Matthias_Buchinger.

WIKIPEDIA. "Origin of the Snow White Tale." Accessed July 26, 2021. https://en.wikipedia.org/wiki/Origin_of_the_Snow_White_tale.

WIKIPEDIA. "Pick-Up Sticks." Accessed July 26, 2021. https://en.wikipedia.org/wiki/Pick-up_sticks.

WIKIPEDIA. "Sarah Biffen." Accessed July 26, 2021. https://en
.wikipedia.org/wiki/Sarah_Biffen.

WILLIAMS, KATHLEEN. *Jonathan Swift: The Critical Heritage*. London: Routledge, 2009.

WINNICOTT, D. W. *Playing and Reality*. London: Tavistock, 1971.

WOOLF, VIRGINIA. "Introduction." *Memoirs of Laetitia Pilkington*.
Ex-Classics. Accessed July 26, 2021. https://www.exclassics.com
/laetitia/lpm003.htm

WORKSHOP OF THE WORLD. "Albert Schoenhut and Company."
Accessed July 26, 2021. https://www.workshopoftheworld.com
/kensington/schoenhut.html.